A GLIDER PILOT BOLD. . . .

by

WALLY KAHN

First published in Great Britain by
Jardine Publishers (1998)
Lasham Airfield
Alton
Hants
GU34 5SR

http://www.jardineaviation.com

Every effort has been made by the author and the publishers to trace owners of copyright material. The events described have been cross-checked wherever possible and the author apologises for any errors or omissions which may have arisen.

Designed and edited by Barry Ketley
Cover artwork by Peter Fuller

ISBN: 0-9534200-0-0

For Margaret—
the best crew chief and co-pilot ever

Contents

Preface

Gliding is the best sport in the world! Whenever and wherever soaring pilots meet, their talk of thermal up-currents and cross-country flights comes thick and fast. Every pilot must tell his own flying stories as not only do they enrich our enjoyment of our sport but also they are a vital teaching aid for the younger, less experienced pilots.

Since 1920, when the sport literally 'took off', there have been three quite distinct phases of development. The pre-war era of trial and error, frustration and very hard physical effort was followed by the post-war expansion and the rapid increase in competitions, cross country flying and the growth of privately owned gliders coupled with the firm re-establishment of gliding clubs. The third phase was the introduction of closed circuit racing in very high performance machines made not of wood, but first of glass fibre and then the even stronger carbon fibre which has totally transformed the sport. The beginner, however, still has to hone his skills on less sophisticated training gliders most of which were also in use in the second phase.

Unfortunately the increasing demands made on the modern racing pilot have, to my mind, had a detrimental effect on the social, clubby atmosphere which prevailed earlier and gave the sport tremendous cohesion and to all pilots a sense of belonging to the same sporting family.

For that reason I have tried to tell some stories about events and people which if not recorded now, will be lost in the fullness of time, which would be a very great pity. If your own favourite story is not included, tell it often and maybe some day another anthology of gliding tales will be produced. My own personal flying stories, like those of other pilots, I keep for long winter evenings in front of a warm fire when my logbooks are produced and nostalgia is king.

Finally I do want to thank the thousands of glider pilots who over the years have made my life so very full and immensely pleasurable. Also I must thank the many patient and kind friends who tried valiantly to make this book almost readable by correcting my prose, grammar, punctuation and stories.

"Tell a story to an average Englishman and he'll laugh three times. The first time is when you tell the joke as he is polite. The second time is when you explain it as he wants to show you that he got the point, and the third time is when he finally sees the joke because he enjoys a good story as well as the next man.

Tell a joke to an average Frenchman and he'll laugh twice. The first time is when you tell it, as he too is polite. The second time is when you explain it as he understands it at once.

Tell a joke to an American and he'll laugh once—when you tell it. Don't waste your time explaining it, he'll never understand your 'strange British humour'.

Tell a story to a glider pilot and before you're half way through, he'll stop you, he has heard a much better version and what the hell do you think you are doing spoiling his story in the first place?.

In the spring of 1894, Albert Liwental, who worked in Dartmouth, became airborne on the slopes above the River Dart in a machine he designed and built himself. This little known achievment, some years before the Wright brothers flew, makes him one of the earliest pioneers of heavier than air flying machines

The Ballad

Words by Pat Wood
Tune: The Airman's lament

A glider pilot bold was he
A maiden unsuspecting she
He landed one day near her home
Demanding tea and telephone

Her dainty heart had missed a beat
Steep turns at five and twenty feet
The field was very very small
The trees were very very tall

But there he was quite safe and sound
Her dainty heart it gave a bound
To see him stand so debonair
The answer to that maiden's prayer

They dallied there for many hours
Among the birds and bees and flowers
And when at last the trailer came
Alas she'd lost her maiden name

What followed it is sad to tell
He drove away as darkness fell
And though devotion he did swear
He soon forgot that maiden fair

Till after many moons there came
A letter headed with the name
Of Swindle, Swindle, Son and Sinn
Solicitors of Lincolns Inn

Dear Sir, our client wishes us
To say that though she wants no fuss
500 smackers more or less
Will keep this matter from the Press

The moral you may clearly see
The ordinary flying fee
Is less expensive than you thought
Compared with other forms of sport.

Chapter I

The early days and Oerlinghausen

I learnt at a very early age that adrenalin was brown.

On Saturday 26 June 1937, as an eleven-year-old, I had gone to the famous Royal Air Force Air Display at Hendon aerodrome in northwest London, the airfield which the early pioneer Claude Grahame-White had created before the First World War. On one small part of what was the airfield is now the home of the RAF Museum which is well worth a visit.

Being then, would you believe, a small thin little boy it was difficult for me to force my way to the front of the crowd in order to get a good view of the proceedings. Being ever foolhardy, I climbed on to a hangar roof without being spotted and thus secured a perfect place from which everything could be seen. When four Kestrel-engined Hawker Fury aeroplanes, then the front-line single-seat fighters in service with the RAF, gave the most exciting display described in the official programme as 'A demonstration of advanced formation flying by a Flight of Four Pilots of No.1 Squadron', everybody watched enthralled. The seven different set pieces consisting of formation changes while performing various aerobatic manoeuvres in very close proximity to each other was a spectacle only equalled to-day by the very best aerobatic teams in the world. When it was over, all applauded including this injudicious enthusiast, who was so carried away with the excitement, that I promptly fell off the roof and impaled my right wrist on an iron railing. The rest of the display was missed as the view from the Station Hospital was non-existent. By a strange quirk of fate, exactly ten years later I was crewing in the National Gliding Championships for Wing Commander Prosser Hanks, then a Pilot Officer in No.1 Squadron, one of the very pilots I had been watching so avidly.

The event that day taught me a valuable lesson–always make certain that you have the best and the safest seat in the house.

If you are afflicted by aviation mania there is really only one cure. Get close to aeroplanes wherever and whenever. At school we had an Avro 504K which was housed on the top floor of the Science Building. It provided me with many happy hours, sitting in the cockpit and pretending that I was flying with Ball, Mannock and Bishop. When the war started, the powers that be decided to move the Avro to a safer location and it was lowered by ropes to the ground. Unfortunately the ropes broke under the strain and a crowd of small boys watched horror stricken as we saw our first "prang".

In the autumn of 1944 a posting to 2 Fighter/Bomber Group, 2nd Tactical Air Force, found me at Hartford Bridge (now called Blackbushe) and then Lasham before rushing through France, Holland and then on to Germany at the end of the war. By then, as I was a very spare bod and a bolshie one at that, some bright spark sent me off to help start a gliding club as a recreation centre for Group personnel. A few miles from the Group Headquarters in Gutersloh is Oerlinghausen, just east of Bielefeld, which had been a well-established wartime gliding school. It was here that the 2 Group Gliding Club now started operations. But we were short of gliders and decided to look for more. We acquired two huge aircraft recovery trailers affectionately known as "Queen Marys" which were towed by three-ton lorries to be used on our raiding parties to find any gliders which had not been smashed. Unhappily both our and the American Governments had decreed that all German military stores were to be destroyed. We arrived at Scharfholdendorf just after twelve empty Kranich two-seaters had been pushed over the side of that wonderful ridge. At an airfield in the American Zone we found thirty Bucker Jungmeister training aeroplanes in a tight circle, all tipped up on their noses about to be burnt by a zealous G.I. We tried to rescue some of the instrument panels but our friendly ally threatened to shoot us if we did not go away. The Americans were very anti-gliding as one of their Colonels had just been killed in a glider and thus their destructive activities were carried out with real enthusiasm. At the Wasserkuppe, they had a field day using machine guns to shoot down gliders hanging in the rafters.

Nevertheless we were very lucky and managed to save about forty assorted gliders which we trailed back to Oerlinghausen. Mark Twomey was the hero of the hour. On one trip he found the Horten IV tailless wonder and persuaded the Americans that, as the whole of the tail section was missing, they might as well let him have the rest as a souvenir. Little did they realise what a prize that flying wing was! Sadly in 1948 our Lords and Masters ordered that it should be handed over to the boffins at the Royal Aircraft Establishment Farnborough who soon afterwards had to give it to the Americans.

In the north of the British Zone, Nos. 83 and 84 Fighter Groups 2nd TAF had started their own gliding club at Salzgitter and very conveniently found an adjacent mine stuffed full of Grunau Babies and other gliders. We at Oerlinghausen came to envy them, for when we ran out of spare gliders, we had to repair ours whereas they just got another one 'out of stock'.

We adopted the well tried and tested German system of solo training which was great fun. As we were not allowed to use German flying instructors, we had to teach ourselves. Needless to say, we cheated and employed such 'Greats' as Pit van Husen who had been the boss of the famed Grunau Gliding Centre during the war, Tasso Proppe, Sepp Niederstadt, Paul Cardinal and that master of the 'squeeze box', Heinz Funk, as notional winch drivers and ground instructors. Some time later I felt rather sorry for them being deprived of their flying, so quite unofficially we let some of them take to the air.

Forty years later, when disguised as a Guernseyman crewing for David Innes at the World Championships in Wiener Neustadt in Austria, Fred Weinholtz of Oerlinghausen and German Aero Club fame introduced me to a group of old German glider pilots each sporting their pre-war dinner plate size Silver or Gold badges. Two came smartly to attention, clicked their heels, shook me warmly by the hand and thanked me for letting them fly back in 1946.

Pit Van Husen did get airborne before the others. A South African parachute major flying a Meise, the glider which had been designed by Hans Jacobs and chosen as the one-class type for the aborted 1940 Olympic Games and later built by France as the Nord 2000 and by Elliotts of Newbury in England as the Olympia, was struck by lightning just as he reached the top of his winch launch. The strike burnt through all the cables and Van Bearle parachuted successfully from only 750 feet, landing on terra firma albeit before the now pilotless Meise. The lightning charge sped down the winch cable, into the winch driven by Pit who was launched upwards to a height of some twenty feet. When he recovered he explained that in truth he preferred flying with wings!

Oerlinghausen was magnificent from every point of view. We could fly as much as we wanted, the site was a great thermal source, we employed superb German craftsmen who maintained our glider fleet and launching equipment beautifully. The social life was something else.

At the end of the war, sad to relate, the black market was king. Looking back on those halcyon days, it must be admitted that we played it for all we were worth and morality did not give us a moment's concern. A cigarette could be sold to tobacco-starved civilians for two shillings and sixpence; for us Servicemen a bottle of whisky cost only twelve shillings and bottles of Pol Roger Champagne even cheaper at eight shillings from the NAAFI stores. Once a week we would play poker and the winner had to stock the bar for the week. As our weekly cigarette ration was 200 Players or Senior Service and we were given a further 40 free Martins 'Non Throat' "nasties" by a shadowy group of well-wishers called 'The Friends of Overseas Servicemen' —the unofficial swap rate was four nasties for every decent cigarette—a week's ration stocked the bar very adequately for all eventualities.

Never fear, your sins will always find you out. On non-flying days it was easy to start the day with the hair of the dog and by lunch the Scotch Whisky Industry export drive was moved up another notch. One day our revered leader 'Jacko' Jackson developed a very painful toothache. Stan Windibank and I took him to a local German dentist who refused to operate as the smell of whisky was too much for him. Not only did he report us to the authorities but we found out later that he was a rabid teetotaller.

Just north of the gliding site is the famous Teutoburger Wald, a low range of hills some seventy kilometres long rising to an average height of two hundred metres along which, on the 15 May 1929, Robert Kronfeld flying his Wien sailplane had established the world distance record of one hundred kilometres. For this feat he won the £250 prize offered by the *Grune Post* newspaper. He found it difficult to cross the gaps in the ridge until he remembered that on previous flights he had found up-currents under clouds and by waiting until suitable ones drifted across his track he was able to complete this epic cross-country. One of our 'Brown Jobs', a friendly though derogatory term applied to our Army members, called Ron Claudi, almost repeated this epic on 22 November 1946. He covered 53 km in 2 hours and 15 minutes and found it equally difficult crossing the long gaps in the range. Although he was flying a Weihe, a modern glider of higher performance than Kronfeld's Wien, the large gap in the hill east of Iburg could not be crossed without thermals. Years later Ron became Canadian Soaring Champion. At the eastern end of the range was the town of Detmold above which stands the Hermanns Denkmal, the large statue of a Germanic folk hero who defeated the Romans; and in the town was the Headquarters of the British Control Commission. We soon established very close and friendly relations with some of the officers who greatly appreciated the Oerlinghausen

'Dolce Vita' and, thanks to them, we were never short of an ample supply of nubile and very impressionable young secretaries eager to attend our parties.

After our dental escapade, the three musketeers running the Gliding Rest Centre were deemed unsuitable and while the other two were nearly time-expired and due to be returned to civilian life, I was banished to Group Headquarters and made to edit the weekly Group Newspaper called *Pinpoint*. As a responsible Editor always looking for contestants for our 'Miss Sundern' beauty contest, it was obviously necessary to interview all new female personnel being posted to us. With that new source of talent we more than made up for the lack of the Detmold beauties for whom Oerlinghausen was now firmly placed 'off limits'.

We always claimed to have invented 'R & R' long before the American forces realised the morale boosting value of 'Rest and Recreation' and developed it into an art form.

25th Anniversary RAFGSA envelope. George Lee, three times World Champion

Chapter 2

More Oerlinghausen

For the vital two years before the end of the war our Air Officer Commanding 2 Group was the wonderful and awe-inspiring Basil Embry. Air Chief Marshal Sir Basil Embry GCB, KCB, KBE, DSO with three bars, DFC, AFC and three Mentions in Depatches had a brilliant Air Force career before the war and then a fantastic war. On the very day in May 1940 when he was supposed to take over RAF West Raynham as Station Commander, he decided to lead his Squadron on a last bombing sortie during which his Blenheim was shot down and he was captured. While escaping he had killed three of his guards which had not made him exactly popular in Germany. The extraordinary story of his escape is well worth reading and an excellent book called *Wingless Victory* by Anthony Richardson chronicles the whole dramatic event. Basil Embry was always the totally dedicated airman and even flew nineteen operations as 'Wing Commander Smith' when he was really an Air Vice Marshal. To get the full measure of the man you must read his autobiography *Mission Completed*.

At the end of the war, it was decided by the Air Ministry that, as the Germans had put a price on his head, he should not be allowed to take his Command to Germany and a new Air Officer Commanding was appointed. It was sad as everyone in the Group loved him but a number of us did rather well from his move. Basil was very fit and always kept himself in great shape. A famous pre-war West End interior decorator serving as a Squadron Leader at Headquarters had selected a splendid mansion in Gutersloh to serve as the A.O.C.'s residence and decided that the bathroom should have a sunken bath with mirrors covering all the walls. When our somewhat portly new bossman took his first bath and saw himself reflected in the mirrors, he ordered their removal and a number of quick thinking opportunists took full advantage of the situation. Two splendid full length dress mirrors graced our room from then on.

By dint of Basil Embry's inspired leadership, 2 Group had a number of outstanding and remarkable senior officers all of whom had distinguished careers during and after the war. One day some of his former senior colleagues decided to have a small select reunion and chose Oerlinghausen as a suitably secure venue. Basil Embry was smuggled in and during the evening's entertainment various traditional RAF mess games were organised. To start proceedings, 'Are you there Captain Moriarty?' came first which calls for two blindfolded worthies lying on the floor each holding the other's left hand while clutching a rolled up newspaper in his right hand. On enquiring whether the said Captain is there, the first contestant has to gauge where the reply came from and deliver a smart blow to what he hopes is his opponent's head. Then it is the other man's turn. The successful blows to various parts of their bodies are counted and after a suitable period of time a winner is declared. Stone cold sober is not the best condition for battle; three parts or more to the wind makes it hugely enjoyable, especially for the onlookers.

2 Group, being a fighter/light bomber unit, the game of Bombers and Ack Ack Guns much played in Bomber Command messes was deemed unsuitable. We were very pleased as we were very short of the requisite equipment. Here a group designated as the Gunners are equipped with full soda water siphons, spaced evenly along the walls but they must lie flat on the floor. The Bombers, each holding a lighted candle in the tail gunner's position must cross the floor on all fours and try to reach the other end without being shot down.

However, High-cock-alorum, a proven method of breaking backs, furniture and spilling blood was followed by a cry for an old fashioned arse kicking contest. Now it so happens that there is an infamous 'Black Mac' somewhere in the Air Force. Who the original model was or indeed why he was so called is lost in the mists of time but every RAF pilot claims to have come up against him. We had our own candidate and Group Captain MacDonald was present that night as well as those splendid RAF twins— the Atcherley brothers—both then Air Commodores. *A Pride of Unicorns* by John Pudney chronicles their amazing progress in the Royal Air Force. Batchy, and his twin David, who was our Senior Staff Officer, were identical and could only be identified by their medal ribbons. Batchy immediately volunteered to start the proceedings with Black Mac as his opponent. Battle commenced and was fast and furious. Neither side was willing to admit defeat and after some time Batchy called for a short respite in order to make room for more drink which was allowed under the rules. After his pee break, he started again with renewed vigour and, after each similar short pause, returned to the fray seemingly fired up more than ever. My hero! What a man! It was only when visiting the holy of holies myself did I see one twin patiently sitting on the throne waiting for the other one to replace him. Black Mac never discovered and lost. Surprise, surprise. You cannot hold good men down and the Atcherley twins were undoubtedly two of the very best.

The next morning after a long night and a hearty breakfast we showed off our gliding activities and Batchy decided that he wanted to fly a Grunau Baby. This did not seem to be a good idea as he could only just fit into the small cockpit and a trip in the two seater Kranich was judged to be more appropriate. However "them what's down below" do not argue with "them what's up above" and thus he climbed into the Baby. With visions of disaster looming and with considerable misgivings I brought the cockpit collar down so forcefully that it caught the top of his head with the wooden cross member which thankfully snapped with a resounding bang and drew blood. "Damn it man" he shouted "are you trying to kill me?". He did not fly that day but later bought me a beer. It was a close call.

We followed the well proven German method of solo training. The student pilot was strapped on to a Primary SG38. This was an open frame device with wings and the pilot sat on a wooden seat totally exposed to the elements. To start he was given ground slides where the driver of the winch pulling him across the airfield ensured that the speed was kept down so that the glider remained firmly on the ground. When the pilot had mastered the technique of keeping his wings level while still on the ground, the speed was increased to allow for low hops. High hops followed and completing seven or eight launches in total including a half turn to the left and then to the right gained him his 'B' certificate. Circuits followed and thereafter he was promoted by being allowed to fly the SG38 with a fairing called 'The Boot' round the nose. No longer did he look past his feet at the ground which, although an improvement for the student, did rather remove the fun of flying this primitive machine. Some dual flights in the Kranich were carried out during this learning period, promotion to the Grunau Baby followed. By then he could call himself a glider pilot.

For the instructors it was heaven. Apart from flying the Kranich, when a pupil landed the SG38 half-way down the field, we would have a fast short winch launch from there, execute a swift 180 degree turn, fly downwind and land back at the take-off point. For high performance flying we had a number of Meises, Weihes (Hans Jacobs' later design), a Mu 13, a Rheinland with retractable landing gear and the gull wing ultra-stable Minimoa, surely one of the most beautiful gliders ever built. Before the war Philip Wills flying his Minimoa was the first pilot in Britain to achieve the Gold 'C' distance flight of 300 km.

The sport of gliding is one which brings out the best in people and encourages human development especially in the young. Yet gliding also appeals to the loner, the introverted as well as the extroverted and we certainly had our share of the latter.

It does not seem proper to describe some of our main players nor would I want to fall foul of our laws of libel but one stands out in the nicest possible way. John, known to all as 'Clue' as he always knew better, was a tall young Army 2nd Lieutenant. He is a lovely man but very prone to putting both feet firmly into his mouth. Rank was ignored on the gliding field and the launch point Controller was second only to the Duty Instructor. When gliders landed, the Controller encouraged other pilots to bring them back to the launch point. Having been well taught by our German friends who believed in hard work being the key to pleasure, Grunau Babies were retrieved by two pilots who would position themselves one under each wing and carry the glider back. An arduous task at the best of times and pilots who landed well down the field were very unpopular.

Our most senior pupil at that time was General Pip Roberts who made up in modesty and charm what he lacked in physical stature. Clue shouted at him to retrieve a Grunau, a command which Pip did not hear. John stormed over to him and gave him the father and mother of all rockets. When he was finished, Pip quietly asked who the young gentleman was. When told, he turned to Clue and said very gently "I understand that you are a 2nd Lieutenant. I am a General. I really would expect you to finish off with Sir!" and with that started walking towards the Grunau. We fell about laughing when we saw Clue running to overtake him shouting "Sir, I will carry it for you, Sir".

There are many stories about Clue then and later. The best was when he was a graduate management trainee in a famous Midlands brewery of which his father was a Director, and he was found lying under a barrel with the tap slightly open so that a steady trickle of beer could enter his mouth without his having to exert himself, just as all the Directors and the principal shareholders were making a tour of inspection. John is now a Baronet and the very model of propriety—more's the pity.

Another worthy was 'Freddie' who was large, dark, sported a splendid handle bar moustache and had a very hairy chest. He was a dashing Observer on Mosquitoes and wore his 'O' half wing Observer's brevet with great pride. When the Air Ministry decreed that 'O' brevets were to be replaced by 'N' for Navigator, Freddie took umbrage and categorically refused to comply. Things got very fraught when the Station Commander told Freddie that unless he did as ordered, hell and damnation would follow. Freddie decided to hide out at Oerlinghausen. One night during a party we decided to lend a hand and shaved off one side of his moustache, his chest and all the way down to his ankle. At first he was not too pleased but suddenly realised that out of defeat could come victory. The next morning he returned to his Station for breakfast, went about his squadron navigation duties as usual and it was not until lunch when the Group Captain walked into the mess and was asked by Freddie for one of the new Brevets to go with his new image that honour was satisfied.

The second time events proved that adrenalin is brown was when on 2 June 1947, Bob 'Peasant' Williams and I had just climbed in cloud to all of 8,400 feet in a Kranich which surprisingly established a new British two-seater height record, the first by members of a RAF Gliding club since the war. We were cavorting in and out of cloud without a care in the world except that both of us desperately wanted to smoke. As my cigarettes were in my trousers, Bob was required to fly nice and gently and especially straight and level as I would have to unstrap myself and fiddle about in my pocket. While doing just that, Peasant suddenly spotted another glider on a close collision course and shoved the stick violently fully forward and to the right. Neither God nor the Devil wanted me that day and I was just able to hang on in the cockpit—but only just! Another valuable lesson learnt, always make certain that all your life support items such as food, sweets, water and fags are readily to hand before take-off.

By May 1947, the now four RAF gliding clubs in Germany decided that it was time to stage a competition. The contestants from each club were divided into two teams, 'A' for experts and 'B' for amateurs and with all the talent we had at Oerlinghausen I just scraped into our 'B' team. Some weeks before the start we had ordered a new trailer for a Weihe from a factory in the very south of Germany. We needed it urgently and had been promised prompt delivery but repeated phone calls to the makers proved less than satisfactory. Then by chance a visitor from the Salzgitter mob whom we regarded as a crowd of cowboys told us gleefully that one of their members had bribed the factory manager to delay collection until after the contest so that we could only field one Weihe against their two. Less than sporting we thought.

On the day before the start, Tasso Proppe and I jumped into our somewhat clapped out Mercedes and sped south driving like the wind. When we arrived at the factory located in a small village, we found it locked and no one around to help. By dint of much bribery and veiled threats of reprisals against the village by RAF bombers, we got our shiny new trailer. On the way back both of us were fit to drop and decided that we should pick up two hitch- hikers who would have to ensure that we did not fall asleep. We saw two young persons of the female gender who seemed admirably suited for our needs and quickly took them on board. Almost at once we got our come-uppance—they had obviously just taken part in the World garlic-eating competition and the pong was indescribable. At the very next Autobahn exit we threw them out but the stench they left behind kept us fully alert for the rest of the journey.

Unlike modern Championships, our rules were very simple. Each day pilots could take off when they liked and the winners were marked on distance flown. On the penultimate day we laid on a 'maxi' Oerlinghausen party and much merriment ensued which continued until first light. The last day dawned grey and overcast and everyone stayed in bed. At 10 o'clock nature called me fairly urgently and having got up, it seemed sensible to go to the launch point to see if anything was happening. In next to no time someone strapped me into my Meise and we soon found some very weak lift. My log book shows a flight of 23 minutes, enough to rush back to our clubhouse and very quietly wake up only our pilots. They all launched and flew-cross country before the weather closed in but our total distance of thirty kilometres won us second place with the hated Saltzgitter entry coming third. Revenge is sweet—let no-one tell you otherwise!

For many months before the contest our craftsmen had been busy repairing and preparing the Horten IV flying wing. We invited the designer Reimar Horten and his chief test pilot Heinz Scheidhauer to Oerlinghausen together with Hanna Reitsch so that they could hopefully pass it airworthy and Scheidhauer to fly it. It was a fantastic moment when he donned his little white flying helmet which looked for all the world like a swimming cap, pushed the goggles on to his forehead and prepared to lie face down in the glider. Wearing goggles even in an enclosed cockpit was a safety precaution he had learnt the hard way. In 1938 during the International Contest at the Wasserkuppe, he and other pilots were caught in a vicious thunderstorm. He was forced to bail out of the Horten 3 he was flying and his barograph showed that he had successfully opened his parachute in violent lift that had, on four occasions taken him up to heights of over 25,000 feet. He was found unconscious in a tree hanging from his parachute harness. He was badly frost bitten and had blacked out through lack of oxygen. When his mother saw him in hospital she could not recognise him. He eventually recovered, losing several fingers to frostbite in the process, and continued to fly tailless aircraft with the Hortens for many years. In those days, pilots attached their barographs to themselves and the trace confirmed his extraordinary ordeal. Some other pilots who were caught in the storm were not so fortunate. He was a quiet, modest and lovely man who only got excited when I pulled his leg about his Silver 'C' badge which looked as if someone had painted a few flecks of gold paint on it. With a hurt expression on his face he said "I have made the Golden height seven times in tailless gliders and the Golden distance three times". I never did learn the wisdom of discretion!

After putting on his backpack parachute, he climbed into the Horten. The pilot lies on his stomach, his chin resting on a leather pad and his feet on pedals behind him. Only fairly small pilots could fit into the cockpit and take-off was full of drama. Captain Eric 'Winkle' Brown, the former Chief Naval Test Pilot and Commanding Officer of the renowned Aerodynamics Flight at the Royal Aircraft Establishment Farnborough describes his flights in the Horten IV in his book, *Wings of the Weird & Wonderful.* The flying demonstration we laid on for our visitors impressed them as much as it did us.

The following year, Jock Forbes, the Chief Instructor of Saltzgitter flew it with hilarious results. Dr. Horten, ever mindful of the pilot 'comfort' requirement had provided a pee-tube built into the fuselage design. However it was essential that the pilot before being strapped down took advantage of the fitting and offered up his vital part in the obvious manner. This Jock did more as a giggle as he was not planning to stay up very long. However on take-off a small leather cover on the outside end of the pipe fell off and a substantial suction was created due to the venturi effect. On landing Jock's comment was " Apart of the extreme discomfort I do not know whether to be pleased or sorry!". Jock later flew for Britain in the 1948 World Championships held in Samedan, Switzerland and on leaving the Royal Air Force, emigrated to America where sometime later he edited *Soaring*, the official magazine of the Soaring Society of America.

In June 1947, the Association of BAFO (British Armed Forces of Occupation) gliding Clubs decided to enter a team in the forthcoming British National Gliding Championship to be held at the Royal Naval Air Station HMS *Gamecock* at Bramcote, Nuneaton, just north of Coventry. The journey from Oerlinghausen, on to Saltzgitter in the north and then through Brussels to the coast was full of incidents though the highlight was undoubtedly our stop in the beautiful town square in Brussels at five in the morning. We found a café just opening and demanded food. "Ham and eggs O.K.?" asked the Patron. The Belgians quite liked the RAF, after all we had presented their famous statue 'Manneken Pis' with a Flight Sergeant Pilot's uniform—quite the funniest parade ever for when the Mayor of Brussels unveiled him suitably clad and the water was turned on, the RAF contingent present burst out laughing and did not appreciate the solemnity of the occasion.

"How many eggs" asked the man. "Twenty four each" shouted our Rhodesian Flight Lieutenant Dave Hughes. It seemed only fair that we forced him to eat a second twenty four egg omelette to make amends but in truth three of us kept him company. Forty-eight eggs later as we were pushing the trailers somewhat precariously along railway lines on to the ship, I fell down between the dock and the side of the boat and was saved just in time by two dockers grabbing my arms. As I write I can hear voices saying "Damn fool dockers, if only they had let him go."

We resolved to show London that the RAF gliding team had arrived. Driving round Parliament Square in convoy was impressive but when we hit Piccadilly Circus at 6 pm on Friday at the height of the rush hour, the effect was hilarious. A circle of covered wagons to fight Indians is one thing but four Jeeps and their long trailers surrounding the statue of Eros which in those days was in the centre of the Circus is something else. Police reaction was almost the same as four years later when members of the Surrey Club circumnavigated Eros with an open tipper truck while we took it in turns to play the very out of tune upright piano that it bore.

The Nationals were great fun. The Chief Marshal was Frank Reade who had just returned to the UK after his stint as officer in charge of Oerlinghausen so that we had a real friend at court. Twenty-six gliders, an entrance fee of three guineas (three pounds and three shillings) with an extra

10 shillings if more than two pilots were nominated to fly. As only Philip Wills (who finally won) and Lorne Welch of the Surrey Club were flying Weihes, then the hottest ships around, we reckoned that with our four Weihes we should do reasonably well. We realised how extremely lucky we were as most of the other competitors had started flying before the war and had to fight hard to re-create their gliding clubs most of which had been stripped of their equipment and even, as in the case of the London Gliding Club at Dunstable, their site. We tried, though not always successfully, not to lord it over the less fortunate pilots with their somewhat less than perfect equipment. The report of the 'Comps' in the August 1947 issue of *Sailplane & Glider* is a gem and must rate with the worst of the worst, or how not to do it.

One day I was standing in front of the prototype Slingsby T.21 two-seater when a small female who was also enthralled by this new monster engaged me in conversation. "How would you like to be a turning point observer? I hear that the organisers are rather short of people". With all the dignity I could muster I explained that I was a crew chief, had a Silver 'C'—still fairly rare in those days—and who the hell was she anyway? That was my first meeting with Ann Welch (then Ann Douglas) and in all the years I have known her she has not changed. Full marks to her, get volunteers even if you have to press-gang them. But more of 'La Tigresse' later.

On one occasion, our pilot, Wing Commander 'Prosser' Hanks, landed in a hamlet called Grafton Underwood. When the crew arrived, we were stopped outside the place by the local policeman who insisted that we follow him. Much to our surprise we were led directly to the 'Pig and Whistle' (the local pub) and there was Prosser surrounded by locals with a large number of pints of beer in front of him. More pints were quickly produced for us and after five or six pints no amount of effort on our part would persuade the locals to release us from this very pleasant captivity. Eventually we won and were ceremoniously escorted to the glider. All became clear when we saw that the local football team had roped it off and were charging interested spectators a fortune just to look at it. How we got home that night without hitting anything is still one of life's great mysteries. The next day Prosser flew but only just managed three miles. We should have stayed, it had the makings of a monumental thrash.

On the final day the then Minister of Aviation, a portly Socialist lawyer called Lord Nathan, was wheeled up to present the prizes. A flying demonstration was arranged in his honour and during the course of it two well known Air Training Corps Instructors flew a Slingsby Gull II with great panache finishing up with a splendid prang slap in front of the VIP which very effectively reduced the two-seater to matchwood. His Lordship was most impressed and thanked the organisation for laying on such an inspiring demonstration crash landing for his benefit. It does seem extraordinary that in successive post war Governments, the Ministerial pecking order ensured that Ministers of Aviation never understood our activities. It proves that we have to be ever alert and ensure that we fight to preserve our freedoms against the machinations of those we respectfully (?) call our 'Lords and Masters'. Our main European competitors appear to be far better served by their elected representatives and are rewarded by official recognition and financial help. The first post-war British Gliding Championships were a great success though only four days proved flyable. The twenty-six gliders together with two Swiss *hors concours* entrants flew a total of 4,376 miles. In those carefree pre-GPS days, distance measuring was not the exact science it is to-day. The entry list reads like a roll of honour of the 'Greats' of pre-war glider pilots with only the young RAF whippersnappers who secured 3rd, 4th and 20th places opening the door for the next generation of competitors to come.

Unfortunately I did not return to Germany with the team and thus missed an action-packed journey back to base. An immediate posting to the BAFO RAF Headquarters to edit the weekly Command newspaper was not welcome as it would undoubtedly interfere with gliding. Quite fortuitously, this assignment did not last too long as I managed to blot my copybook most effectively. It so happened that in Buckeberg there was a Schloss which was owned by some distant relations of our Royal Family. One night this imposing edifice caught fire and as many airmen as could be found were brought in to rescue anything of value from the blaze. Needless to say a number of them soon discovered the well stocked wine cellar and quickly found that there were far too many bottles and it was much more efficient to empty a number before making the perilous and exhausting journey up the hundreds of stairs to the outside world. After a number of these sorties some airmen were quite 'tired' and felt the need to lie down on the grass where it was even easier to sample the precious nectar.

The entire editorial staff of the 'BAFO Times' consisting of a photographer and the Editor arrived in time to record a very irate Assistant Provost Marshal, one Wing Commander Harry Stonard, pointing at each drunken airman and putting him on a charge. Quite naturally he did not take kindly to our activities and when we explained that our pictures of the fire were fairly commonplace but our action shots of him would make a superb story which we hoped would make the British National press, he ordered us to leave at once but first tried unsuccessfully to get hold of our film. He complained to higher authority and all three of us were swiftly moved to other duties. By a strange coincidence, much later Harry and I were colleagues in the tobacco industry and he agreed to forgive me for the incident. For me it was a blessing in disguise because it enabled me to spend the last six months in the Service gliding virtually full time, first at Mindeheide and then at Scharfholdendorf.

Hard work is the key to pleasure

Chapter 3

Mindeheide and Scharfholdendorf.

On arriving at Mindeheide, a flat site in the Minden gap, I was immediately taken to task by one Group Captain Christopher Paul, a very forceful and gallant former 2 Group Mosquito Squadron Commander who had taken charge of all gliding in the Command. We had met before when, soon after arriving in Germany, he had visited us at Oerlinghausen and had taken a launch in our very special Weihe which we had 'buffed up' ready for the forthcoming British Nationals at Bramcote. As he had never before experienced a 'centre of gravity' launch (where the winch cable is attached to a hook well down the fuselage which enables the pilot to climb very steeply), it was deemed prudent to use the nose hook which generally produced a pathetic launch. This did not work out as it should and he, the Weihe and the ground met in a manner not befitting the new boss of all gliding. Our beautiful Weihe—we were not best pleased and in truth neither was he! He quite correctly assessed the state of play in our little world and announced that changes for the better would be made. He then left to leave us to contemplate the fact that life would never be the same again.

"You work here, teaching pilots to fly. Very few thermals to distract you, so get on with it" he said. It was solo training supervision with two-seater checks in the Kranich whenever possible. We made our pupils sweat and each newcomer before starting his training was made to produce forty feet of tacking strips which were used to secure scarf joints during repairs. They had to cut long narrow strips of plywood and gently hammer in small nails every three inches along their length. It says a lot for our training methods that after a few months we had enough to keep the world gliding movement sated for the rest of time.

The womenfolk, who in those pre-politically correct days were called 'Camp followers' now more kindly described as 'Gliding Widows', were pressed into sandwich and tea-making and kept us happy. One of my young pupils was a motor mechanic Corporal called Andy Gough who had a severe linguistic communication problem with his German girl friend Trudie. As she was our champion sandwich maker, I was pressed into service as their interpreter and had to persuade Andy to learn German so that he could communicate in time for the forthcoming arrival of young Andy. In the mid-eighties, young Andy became the Canadian soaring champion, which would have delighted his father who was sadly killed on 12 June 1981 at Brize Norton in a tragic gliding accident while giving one of his fabulous aerobatic displays. 'Old' Andy Gough developed into one of the 'Greats' of British gliding. From 1948 until his death, he was the charismatic Chief Gliding Instructor of various BAFO and Royal Air Force Gliding and Soaring Association clubs and eventually made the RAF centre at Bicester his personal fiefdom of excellence and performance. With Derek Piggott, he rates as the very best instructor to whom countless glider pilots owe an enormous debt of gratitude. Andy was an entrepreneur par excellence, always looking for a deal from which he invariably came out on top. An American friend of mine who had been cheated by a less than honest art dealer said philosophically "If you are landed with lemons, you've got to make lemonade!" When I told Andy the story he said "Never happened to me, just as well, I don't like lemonade". He treated everyone the same, regardless of their rank and was universally loved by all who came into his world.

Mindeheide was hard work, satisfying and fun. Chris Paul came up with some strange ideas, one of which was to fit a loudspeaker on the frame of the open SG38 above the pupil's head so that we could radio instructions to him in the air. Thankfully the scheme never got off the ground as we could never make the radio work. After a few weeks a rare opportunity to fly a Grunau came my way and my request to attempt a cross-country to my old club was met with considerable derision from certain quarters. It was with great pleasure when later that day we telephoned from Oerlinghausen requesting a retrieve.

Scharfholdendorf, also known as 'Der Ith', was something else. A fantastic hill-top site, the main ridge is an outcrop of limestone over twelve miles long which you could hill-soar on both sides. The West ridge is over 600 feet high for most of its length and was certainly the most spectacular and one of the finest ridges you could hope to find anywhere in the world. The Germans had built a splendid holiday complex on top complete with swimming pool, tennis courts and all the comforts of home. A gliding club completed the amenities. On the main side of the hill they had even built a light railway so that gliders landing in the valley below could be put on a trolley and winched back up to the top. Unfortunately, at the time of the great Kranich destruction party by the zealous official vandals, the railway had suffered the same fate as the gliders. When our pupils were deemed competent pilots, they transferred from the flat site at Mindeheide to the much more challenging narrow strip at Scharfholdendorf. When the west wind was strong, we used a very short launch run at a right angle to the hill. On light wind days the winch cable was laid out along the hill.

Early on Chris Paul decided to organise the first BAFO Instructors course so that training methods could be standardised, which very nearly ended my gliding career prematurely. He sat in the front seat of the Kranich and yours truly was ordered to fly him round acting as the Instructor. On landing he seemed satisfied and insisted that we swap roles and seats. When we landed he asked for my comments and joking I suggested that he needed to have more dual. Yet another valuable lesson learnt the hard way—humour should be severely restrained when dealing with senior officers.

We taught advanced flying in the Kranich which included aerobatics. We gave aerobatic displays at the week-ends to entertain the multitude who used the rest centre for various recreational activities and to attract new members. If the wind was on the hill it allowed you to do repeated very low passes over the swimming pool and tennis courts which stood you in good stead later with highly impressionable young ladies. Apart from loops, spins and chandelles one popular manoeuvre was the full blown tail slide in a Kranich or Grunau Baby. Why and how we never had a single case of elevator hinge or total glue failure is a mystery. It is a stupid thing to do and attempted to-day in modern gliders would certainly result in the pilot being thrown out of the Brownies!

One problem, we never overcame no matter what we did. Every Kranich was equipped with an undercarriage consisting of two wheels and a short axle which was attached to the fuselage by two lugs. By pushing a small lever in the cockpit, the pilot could jettison this on take-off and land on the skid which resulted in a shortened landing run. We hated having to lift the back of the fuselage in order to relocate the wheels and tended to fly with them on. Inevitably some visitors or pupils in moments of slight panic would push the lever and away would go the wheels. Some four hours after a glorious hill soaring flight during which one of those infuriating twits had dropped our wheels from a height of three thousand feet, a German farmer arrived at the site and explained that he was ploughing one of his fields when he heard a 'bomp'. He looked up but saw nothing so he went back to work. Soon after there was another 'bomp' and again he saw nothing. Then there were lots of 'bomps' and lo and behold at his feet was the undercarriage. He explained that he was quite used to finding Kranich wheels on his farm and added that before and during the war he was always rewarded with a bottle of Steinhager. As he was wearing the most fabulous hat, we soon did a deal. He went off happy with two bottles of whisky and I acquired our wheels and the thermal hat of all time which was worn on every flight until someone pinched it during the 1955 Nationals.

On the 13 September 1947 the weather looked superb with lots of tight cumulus clouds over the site which showed promise of building into big ones in the afternoon. The Group Captain had telephoned to tell us that he would come after lunch and to reserve our only serviceable Weihe. Past experience had taught us that you did not willingly cross our revered leader and so at 13.15 hours I took a launch in a Grunau Baby which was not equipped with any blind flying instruments. I sat above the site, cursing my luck when at last after an hour I saw the staff car arrive, drive straight past the launch point and on to the middle of the woods beyond the site, a place which was tailor made for other forms of sport. Hoping that himself and friend would probably be happily engaged for some time, I opened the dive brakes, landed near the Weihe, jumped in and took off. After just over an hour I was back on the ground being given a monumental rocket by an irate Group Captain for pinching his glider. When the storm had blown itself out, I meekly produced the barograph which showed an 11,000 foot climb which was enough for our first Gold 'C' height and promised that it would never happen again. In fairness he was very good about it but it was just as well that my demobilisation date was only three months away.

My last flight was back at Oerlinghausen and that night and the two next ones for good measure a number of us leaving the Service were dined out in great and very liquid style. No one can hope to go to Heaven twice. I was lucky—the previous two and half years was the first visit. The next was to start on 20th December 1947 in the red Slingsby Cadet above Dunstable Downs in Bedfordshire and has continued ever since.

Chapter 4

Dunstable and Redhill

The Sailplanes taken from ***The Trackless Way*** by Leonard Taylor:

How gentle are the sailplanes,
They do not crash or burn,
Much cheaper than the mailplanes,
And easier to learn,
And silent over Dunstable's long hills they go in flight,
Like sleepy rural constables,
Patrolling through the night

On a short duty trip to England in August 1947 time allowed a quick visit to the Surrey Gliding Club site at Redhill aerodrome. At that time the Surrey Club had a fleet consisting of a Cadet, a Tutor, four Olympias and a Weihe and the presiding genius as resident Chief Instructor was Lorne Welch. P.P.L.E.Welch was one of nature's genuine characters. A relation by marriage had been the great practical joker Horace de Vere Cole who indulged in numerous splendid japes. One was to stand on a corner of a building near the Bank of England in the City of London and stop a proper 'City Gent'—in those far off days wearing a dark suit, white shirt, stiff collar, bowler hat, gloves and carefully rolled umbrella. He would explain that he was measuring the building and asked whether said 'Gent' could just hold the end of his tape measure whilst he went round the corner. He would then find another volunteer to hold the other end. He then crossed to the opposite side of the road and watched to see how long they stood their ground. He once succeeded in having three buildings being 'measured' at the same time! His most famous act was to dress up as the Sultan of Zanzibar and successfully persuaded the Admiralty to arrange for him to review the Fleet lying off Spithead. Apparently when they discovered the truth, their Lordships were less than pleased.

The stories about Lorne, told by him or of him are all true and most amusing. His wife Ann should be persuaded to write his biography so that future generations will be able to read about his fascinating life.

At the start of the war he was a flying instructor in the RAF and one day was detailed to ferry a Tiger Moth from an airfield in Scotland to Brough in the North of England. On the way, he decided to break his journey and visit some family friends. He landed in a field near their house and after being given tea by his host was persuaded to stay the night. A maid took his sparse luggage to a bedroom and when he went up to change for dinner he found that she had quite properly laid out his clothes but was obviously fooled by the parachute. She had taken it out of the bag and carefully placed it on a chair with the straps decorously draped over the side.

After a long stint instructing, he managed to join Bomber Command only to be shot down soon after. The story of his escape with Walter Morison from their prison camp, and of the famous tunnel in Stalag Luft III and then Colditz are fully chronicled in Walter's book *Flak and Ferrets*; it is very well worth reading. The Surrey Club was a thriving vibrant organisation and on handing over a cheque my membership was accepted there and then. I asked Lorne if there was anything he wanted which could be 'liberated' and brought back from Germany. As he was dreaming of designing the perfect winch which he had decided to build and later completed, he asked for the rollers, paying on gear and guillotine mechanism off a Pfeiffer winch. Five months later, having carried the heavy crate back which meant leaving a 56 piece Furstenberg dinner service behind as we were severely limited in how much 'loot' could be brought home, I arrived in the middle of the Surrey Club Christmas party which was in full swing in the clubhouse. With great aplomb the crate of goodies was deposited on the floor in front of Lorne. "Hi, here is what you wanted" I said and waited expectantly for his reaction. "Oh, what's that then" he asked and then added "just put it in a corner somewhere". No word of thanks or appreciation. The very next day in a childish pique, I drove to Dunstable and joined the London Gliding Club. To-day I know better. Lorne was quite right, why thank someone for doing something for the common good, just doing it is enough reward.

Surrey and London Clubs could not have been more different in attitude. The Surrey Club had been joined in 1947 by the Imperial College of Science and Technology Gliding Club which was established in 1930 and is thus the oldest University Club in the country. Apart from a few notables, the members at Redhill were predominantly pilots who were too young to have flown before or during the war and satisfied their burning ambition to fly by learning to glide as power flying, although much cheaper than to-day, was beyond their meagre financial means. Thus the spirit and general 'get up and go' attitude to gliding and life in general together with a cross-country flying culture actively encouraged and fostered by Lorne Welch was very stimulating. Two innovations of his which were much admired and later copied by some other clubs were the introduction of dual training and then first solos in 'Daisy' our Slingsby T.21 and the very popular 'cry Joe' scheme. At the start of the season, every soaring pilot was given the opportunity of selecting a specified date on which an Olympia or even our flagship the Weihe could be booked all day. If the Gods smiled on the day selected, the fortunate 'Joe' could attempt a cross-country or just use the aircraft for local soaring. In those days before private ownership became the fashion it taught us all a valuable lesson in task selection and decision making.

The London Club at Dunstable on the other hand still had a large number of pre-war pilots and the Committee found it difficult to understand the attitude and aspirations of the young. Even noisy social activities were discouraged and were felt not to be in keeping with their rather staid outlook. Slope soaring up and down the Dunstable ridge seemed to be favoured by most of the pilots and flying cross-country was a comparative rarity. A few years later however, Frank Foster by his example actively encouraged members to fly cross-country. His simple message was "if there are thermals over the site, then there will be thermals further away—so go and find them!". Frank, a Captain flying for British European Airways, was Nick Goodhart's co-pilot in the 1956 World Championships held in France when they became the World Two-Seater Gliding Champions. Very sadly he was killed when his airliner on a flight near Italy was torn apart by a military fighter aircraft. Much later John Jefferies, then the Chief Instructor at Dunstable pioneered the 'lead and follow' cross-country training scheme, where flying a two-seater with a pupil, he led other pilots flying single seaters on declared tasks. This has proved to be an excellent system designed to give greater confidence and to improve the skills of younger pilots.

To digress, before winches were adopted as the preferred and the most effective method of launching, the bungey reigned supreme. The glider was perched on the edge of the hill and a ring was placed round a hook under the nose. Two thick rubber shock cords attached to short ropes were then pulled tight by the bungey crew of four people on each side forming a 'V' and on the command 'walk' they would start off down the hill until the bungey was nearly fully stretched and after the shout of 'run' when the bungey was fully stretched, the glider shot off into the wide blue yonder. For the pilot it was always a magic moment, for the crew it was very hard work. Pulling the glider back up the hill for the next pilot was even harder work and some clubs including the Dunstablites found horses very effective for this purpose. One day a bright spark suggested using the horses as the bungey crew as volunteers were hard to find. The slope is not very steep, horses don't pay an annual subscription so they thought they'd give it a go. Horses do not understand plain English and soon found themselves going downhill rather fast. Before anyone could stop them, the bungey broke and each horse was hit smartly on his rear with a resounding crack. Story has it that it took Tim Hervey the Chief Instructor three days before he found and retrieved the horses from quite a distance away. A pulley system was soon substituted and was found to be much more reliable, providing that the 'look-out' man remembered to shout 'stop' before the glider reached the pulley at the top of the hill.

Like all gliding clubs, Dunstable had its share of colourful characters. One stands out above all the others and as the result of one of his exploits has given a name to a grass field. He is Archie Erskine, a famed psychiatrist who was ever eager to fly. Very early one bright morning with the wind blowing on the hill, he persuaded a fellow member to give him a winch launch well before any of the others had even left their warm beds. Clad only in his pyjamas, off he went to soar the hill. Making his way down to the Whipsnade Zoo end of the ridge, he flew happily for a time until, suddenly, the wind dropped. With no hope of getting back to the site, he landed in a suitable field, walked to the nearest house to telephone the club. On being woken by loud banging on her front door and confronted by a man dressed only in his pyjamas was not the way to make friends and influence people. Smartly banging the door in his face, she telephoned the police demanding protection. It was only after Archie had shown the lady of the house and the local policeman his glider, that he was able to telephone for a retrieve. To this day, that field is called 'The Pyjama Field'.

Archie was also determined to complete his 300km distance flight for the coveted 'Gold C' badge. Always declaring Plymouth airfield in Devon as his goal, on his numerous abortive attempts he must have landed in every field on track within 30 miles of Dunstable. It was the standing joke that whenever the telephone rang in the clubhouse, people would shout "It must be Archie, where has he landed now?" One cloudless day when hardly anyone bothered to get airborne, off went Archie and many hours later telephoned having reached his goal at last. The story has it that he hardly climbed higher than 2,000 feet over the whole distance. Quite a man.

Even newly joining trained glider pilots were required to fly at least five hours in Cadets and Tutors before being considered for anything of better performance. It was a joy to visit Redhill to be able to fly Olympias and the Weihe. Later at Dunstable Dan Smith, then the Chairman of the Flying Committee, took pity on me and ordered their somewhat strange Resident Instructor Hugh Wheatcroft to let me fly anything and to start instructing as well. My log book records flights in various gliders including the tiny Baynes Scud II which has a wing span of 12.9 metres, an empty weight of 68kg and when new in 1932 cost £150 ex-works Farnham, Surrey. As I was still quite slim, though tall, getting into the Scud was a difficult exercise which, fifty odd years later at almost twice the weight of the glider would be downright laughable. The Zlin Krajanek, an up to date aerobatic Czech design loosely based on the Grunau Baby, in which Ladi Marmol established the British Duration record on the hill at Dunstable of over 33 hours, was a joy to fly. The highlight was undoubtedly taking Joan Price's sister and Joan's young daughter for an hour's hill soaring in the prototype T.21 affectionately called 'The Barge' which had a cockpit large enough to hold the three of us. In to-day's regulated and very protective society, this caper would not be allowed under any circumstances.

Gliding, the sport of silent flight is magic. Everyone should try it. Flying in an open cockpit machine on a glorious summer's day is sheer bliss, cavorting with soaring birds and occasionally meeting the odd butterfly which has been taken aloft by a column of warm rising air, the life blood of all soaring aficionados; but one does have to remember that voices carry. Once flying with the beautiful Diana, I suggested a loop in the T.21. Panic stricken at the thought she shouted "No, Wally No!". Convincing friends on the ground afterwards that only a simple loop was on offer was no easy task. John Free who was the Army Club's resident Instructor in the early days of Lasham had a more torrid time. When flying over Lasham village, he admonished his pupil rather too forcibly ending the tirade with "You are a bloody fool, that's what you are". Later that day the Vicar of the charming Lasham church which was built on the site of a Saxon church, came to the club complaining that as he was trying to compose his sermon for the following day he did rather object to the heavenly castigation booming out from above.

Dunstable is Dunstable

The Glider Pilot's Psalter, produced on Ascension Day 1939 by the Lay Brethren of St.Hucklow Priory, Higher Winchum

Won't you come into our clubhouse
So modern and so spry?
Where many famous pilots eat
And tell us how they fly

Oh, please don't talk so loudly
Your tone must humble be
Did I understand you rightly, Sir
You've only got a 'C'?

Yes quite! Of course! We must take care
So pleased you understand
For Dunstable is Dunstable
No! We haven't got a band

I beg your pardon? Yes, you're right!
That sure is Ashwell Cooke
You know him then? How very odd
Of course, you've read his book?

You know, of course, we've a Golden 'C'
It's in that glass case there
By all the hills here's Philip Wills!
Just bask, it's rude to stare

What's that, you ask, upon the wall
Revolving Chart and Box?
Oh, that's a Cloud Base Instrument
Designed by Mr. Fox

This picture here "The Times" called weird
It caused no end of fuss
'Tis "Minimoa" thousands up

Yes, that is the Octopus

Yes, it's quite the Temple of the Great
Your description's very neat
Good Heavens above! You'll pardon me
But you haven't wiped your feet!

Under Lorne Welch's dynamic tutelage the Surrey club was the most successful soaring club in the country with a strong emphasis on cross-country flying. After one glorious flight over south London, then over Westminster Bridge the thermals gave out and a landing was made at Brentford in Essex. On the way home with retrieve car and trailer we stopped at a lorry driver's café, then the ideal pull up for glider drivers. "What have you got in that trailer" asked the café owner. On being told he said "Ah! you are the brassiere boys, you harness the uplift". His next merry quip I have used often since then when trying to raise funds for our sport "Gliding! It's the sport without visible means of support."

Expeditions to other sites were encouraged and in August 1948 four of us drove to a French gliding centre at Challes-les-Eaux near Chambery in Southern France. The flying was spectacular but we made the mistake of teaching the French pillow fighting and a drinking game called 'Cardinal Puff'. Some years later when visiting another centre at Pont St.Vincent near Nancy in north eastern France, we discovered that French glider pilots had taken both to their hearts but demanded that we perform 'Cardinal Puff' in French and Green Chartreuse! With typical Gallic panache they altered the art of pillow fighting, the end came not when the contestants were tired or bored but only when all the pillows had been demolished and all concerned were covered in feathers.

The social life at Redhill left nothing to be desired. As well as a popular squash court nearby, we had built a cosy snug bar in the corner of the clubhouse. The Surrey Flying Club had a well appointed bar for their wealthier members a hundred yards from ours and the RAF Volunteer Reserve unit had their mess some twenty yards further on. It was a case of 'throttle to bottle' in a very meaningful way.

Our parties enlivened the long winter evenings and were always well attended with visitors coming from near and far. One evening a fancy dress party was arranged with all participants having to wear something with an aeronautical theme. Tony Goodhart came as a CuNb (a cumulo-nimbus or thunderstorm cloud for the uninitiated) wearing a strange structure made of cotton wool on his head. In the centre a lighted candle served as a lightning strike but inevitably his magnificent creation was soon fully alight! Tony Oram pinned a blanket to his shoulders with a note on his navel announcing that he was a warm front. There were many more ingenious costumes. John Sowrey, later an Air Commodore in the RAF and the son of one of the famous Sowrey Brothers cheated a bit by arriving in his Father's First World War Royal Flying Corps uniform albeit with the right trouser leg cut vertically to provide room for the plaster cast from toe to knee acquired on a recent Surrey Club Skiing expedition to Switzerland. As a member of the RAFVR unit, I suggested that a visit to their dining-in shindig being held that night might liven things up so off we went. The Commanding Officer and his guests cheered or booed depending on our costumes but John held back as he wanted to make the grand entrance. Flinging open the door with such gusto that it nearly came off its hinges, he shouted "I say you chaps, can some of you help—I have just pranged my Camel". Unfortunately the very old Air Commodore who was an honorary member of the Mess, on seeing this apparition and hearing the shout, fainted clean away.

Our parties were, to say the least, always full of surprises. As the weather before one Christmas party promised extreme cold, no hell but plenty of damnation. The punch provided was of the 'get that down you, it'll warm you up in a trice' variety, The ingredients consisted of twelve bottles of brandy, thirty six bottles of red wine, a large tin of treacle, brown sugar, a few herbs and spices and lastly about ten pints of strong cider to 'water it down a bit!' Members contributed whatever they felt would add to the festivities and that year a frightfully clever Imperial College member called Dr. Maggie Thornley donated a vast quantity of 'Mars' bars which some bright spark cut into thin slices. When asked why he did it he said that as it would be the only time in his life when he could be beastly to two hundred Mars all at once, he could not resist! Weird members!! Maggie explained that having once conducted some piece of scientific research on a chocolate related problem, she had been asked to be a 'Mars' Bar Taster and every week a large parcel arrived, the contents of which she was supposed to eat and return her tasting findings to the manufacturer. Another member brought a sack full of peanuts. He had come home on leave from Africa where he was running the 'Groundnut scheme'. This was an attempt by the post-war Labour Government to combine overseas aid with an increase in food production, employment and increased stability in an African country. By the time the project was cancelled, the cost was more than even our Masters were willing to fund. We reckoned that the large sack in our possession had cost the British tax payers its weight in gold. The night of the party, only 45 hardy souls appeared and were give some punch on arrival. When after a splendid thrash we woke up the next morning feeling a little older, we discovered that some kind soul had thrown the uneaten Mars bar slices and the peanuts into the punch bowl which still contained a fair amount of the precious liquid. As breakfast the mixture was delicious!

Expeditions to other clubs around the country were looked forward to with eager anticipation as they provided varied and interesting flying and of course the opportunity to cause mayhem at which we were very adept. At the Southdown site at Friston near the coast in Sussex we gave our hosts our 'Austin Seven Spectacular' where the five examples of this wonderful motor car owned by various members would be driven round in a tight circle, hand throttles set and the owners would then jump out and leave the cars to it until inevitably disaster loomed and the owners had to mount their chariots in the best way they could. Hugo Trotter always maintained a large supply of tinned food in his Austin for these expeditions but in time all the labels came off the tins. Heating or not heating was therefore a lottery although after a hard day's flying, hot peaches in syrup or cold vegetable soup tasted equally delicious.

40th anniversary RAFGSA envelope. John Delafield, eight times UK National Champion

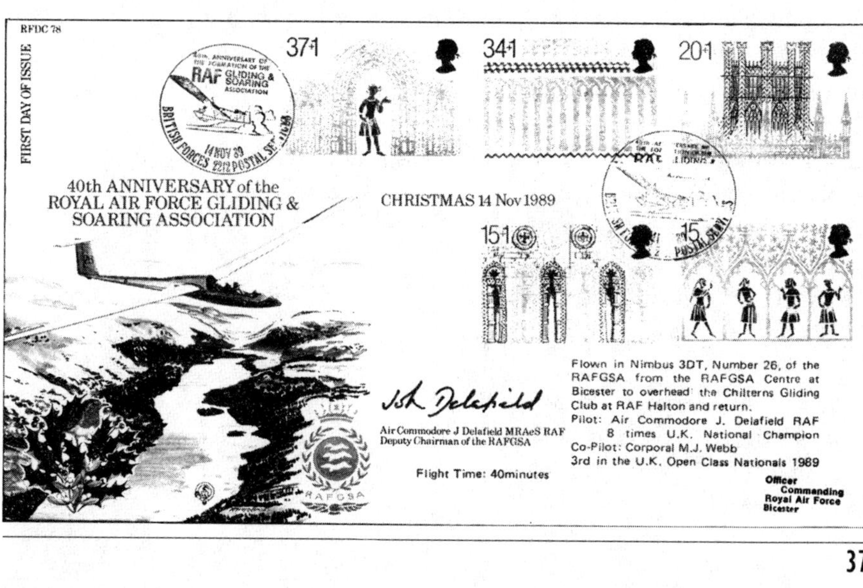

Chapter 5

The Mynd and the Cambridge Club

In 1949, we were exposed to the Cambridge University Gliding Club annual expedition to the Midland Club site perched on the top of the Long Mynd south of Shrewsbury in Shropshire. In general the Cantabrians were a splendid bunch, high IQs, great sense of adventure but some just downright foolhardy. Their annual visitations to this magnificent hill top location from which you get a wonderful view westwards towards Wales was always a marathon. They seemed to bring all their worldly gliding goods with them, towed by a collection of runcible vehicles which defied description. In keeping with their attitude to life and a total disregard of officialdom, it was quite normal for the least experienced undergraduate to be entrusted with the most arduous task. Alan Purnell well remembers towing two gliders on one trailer with the Cambridge tractor, a journey taking two days which was just as well as not only had he no driving licence, he had never driven anything before. The experience did him no harm though he much prefers cross-country gliding. By the end of 1997 he had flown for more than 8,500 hours in sailplanes, completed 572 flights of over 300km and 109 flights of over 500km, virtually all of them in the United Kingdom.

Cambridge Club stories are numerous, very funny, but some like many good gliding tales, possibly a trifle apocryphal. The authenticity of the following ones have been checked with my contemporaries—but as with all old men, it is the memory that goes first and as Lee Trevino the golfer once said "the older I get, the better I used to be!". In those far off days, the Midlanders referred to their home as 'The Mecca of British Gliding'.

The Fumblies
—with apologies to Edward Lear.
History shows the author as 'Anon'!

They went to soar at the Mynd, they did
At the Mynd they went to soar
In spite of all that their friends could say
On a winter's morn, on a stormy day

At the Mynd they went to soar

The anemometer went slowly round
And keen types were anxious to get off the ground
"Though we go to the bottom and have to derig
We don't care a button, we don't care a fig
To the Mynd we've come to soar"

Chorus
For far too few, far too few
Are the days with a Westerly wind
And they didn't go there to look at the view
They went to soar at the Mynd

He flew away in the Pons, he did*
In the Pons he flew so far
"If I shut my eyes and pretend I'm brave
I may catch up with a standing wave
(They will fetch me back with a car)"

But his friends cried out as they saw him go
"He's a clot to go up in the clouds, you know
For the sky is dark and the wind is strong
And happen what may, it's extremely wrong
In the Pons to fly so far"

He tried to soar a Cadet, he did
To soar a Cadet he tried
But he started off at terrific pace
"Does he think he is going in for a race?
He will go to the bottom" they cried

When approaching to land over trees of great height
There came an abrupt termination of flight
For the downdraught had got him and pulled him below
The other chaps murmured "It just goes to show!"

*The much loved 'Pons' was the the Dart Aircraft Ltd Cambridge 1, built at Dunstable and first flown in 1935.

As they shovelled the wreckage aside

He went to fly on a test, he did
On a test he decided to fly
To demonstrate to the pupils there
A Cadet couldn't possibly stay in the air
(So he didn't get very high)

This demonstration of carelessness
Was watched by the others with some distress
He scraped the hills as he flew along
Yet he never thought he was rash or wrong
Till he fell out of the sky!

Far too few, far too few
Are the days with a westerly wind
And although they really haven't a clue
They've been to soar at the Mynd

The Midland Club hangar is a splendid steel structure which looks for all the world like a miniature rainbow stuck on the top of the hill. Taking the gliders out in the morning and putting them back at the end of flying was a great 'tour de force' presided over by Teddy Proll their resident engineer. Shouts of " everybody lift" and "everybody push" could be heard by half the county as Teddy made us thread yet another wing over one and under another. Hangar packing was an art form which only he ever fully understood.

One evening a number of the Cambridge members decided to sleep on top of the curved hangar roof and needless to say discovered that man tosses and turns when asleep. It is said that drunks seldom hurt themselves when falling down which is certainly not the case when you roll off from the top of the Mynd's pride and joy.

The Chairman of the Midland Club then was Charles Wingfield, a quite splendid 'one off' character of the old school. He had just taken delivery of his shiny new Olympia and very generously allowed a number of us to fly his previous glider, a Slingsby Kirby Kite I called ' Gracias' known affectionately as 'Grassy Arse'. In 1947 Charles had been a member of the British team flying in the American National Soaring Contest held at Wichita Falls in Texas. This event attracted seventy sailplanes and lasted for fifteen days. Apart from setting new British Distance and Out-and-return records flying an Olympia, he also gained the second Gold 'C' on the British register.

However he will be remembered by the Americans for something quite different. Charles was a tall distinguished looking man, sporting a full moustache and during the Contest habitually wore his wartime Army khaki desert gear—during the war he saw much service in North Africa including a spell as ADC to General Sir Alan Cunningham, the General Officer Commanding East Africa Force. To the Americans he was the model English Gentleman and it is possible that the late very funny actor Terry Thomas modelled himself on Charles. For the last two days of the meet the hosts were rushing about like demented flies and there was great hustle and bustle. The activity was meant to be a great secret but you cannot keep anything quiet on a gliding site. Came the last evening and Captain Ralph Barnaby, US Navy (Rtd), the President of the Soaring Society of America, took Charles by the arm and led him to a site where ox and pig roasting as well as a mountain of T-bone steaks were being prepared in great profusion. "This Sir" said the gallant Captain, with a theatrical sweep of his arm "is in your honour". Charles surveyed the scene, waited until he had everyone's rapt attention and then said "Oh I say, what is it?". "A genuine Texas barbecue" was the answer. "Oh I say" said Charles "how jolly primitive".

He lived a full and interesting life, always active in outdoor pursuits as well as distinguished service to the community, serving not only as the High Sheriff of Shropshire but also a Justice of the Peace and Chairman of the Mid-Shropshire Bench. He lived near the Long Mynd in the family house which was a sort of mini-Buckingham Palace. It was very much the stately home built on the estate owned by the family since 1753. Even earlier, several Wingfields held offices of State during the reign of King Henry VIII and were named in the King's Suite at the Field of the Cloth of Gold. An illustrious family—one ancestor helped to teach the Swiss to ski and a great uncle of Charles, Walter Clopton Wingfield, was the 'father' of lawn tennis. Charles was an enthralling colourful human being who kept us amused by his many true life stories. In one he recalled that the only serious injury he sustained in the fighting in the Low Countries in 1940 was during his evacuation from Dunkirk aboard a fishing boat where he suffered sunburn to the soles of his feet after snoozing barefoot during the arduous journey back to England. The address of his family home said it all. Even the Post Office delivered letters addressed simply to 'Onslow, Shropshire'. While we were at the Mynd we were invited to visit him there and when his man-servant general factotum called Anson opened the door to us he asked us who we were. On being told that we were his Master's gliding friends, he led us directly to the downstairs toilet pointing out the soap and towels in a very obvious fashion. Charles had a great sense of humour and enjoyed doing the unexpected. On one occasion he appeared at Redhill in full morning dress complete with a grey top hat and insisted on flying our Slingsby Tutor open cockpit as he wanted to see whether he could complete the flight without losing his hat!

Another Wingfield story regretfully David Ince omitted from his autobiography (he claims there just was not space!) concerns the Leaders and Elders of the Derby & Lancs Gliding Club who took themselves rather seriously. The younger pilots attending an early post-war National Championship being held at Camphill made every effort to liven up the proceedings. Charles, then Chairman of the Midland Club, challenged David Ince, his Chief Flying Instructor, to a duel. Both attired in their pyjamas, Charles's being made of pure silk, were required to expel their natural gases from a certain part of their anatomy while holding on to a tree near the clubhouse. The gas was lit and the one producing the longest flame was adjudged to be the victor. The young thought it a great joke though it took some time before the Elders stopped muttering about smutty schoolboy pranks and the state of the modern world!

On our first morning at the Mynd, Doctor Cotton arrived in his Bradford Jowett van and persuaded Charles to give him a check flight in their Slingsby T.21. Charles had just rigged his Olympia and was eager to fly as the local hunt was active at one end of the hill and he wanted to 'put on a bit of a show' for them. The story goes that his beat up was not really appreciated by the hunt although when in 1952 he was forced to stop gliding due to the debilitating recurrence of severe sinusitis from which he had suffered for some time, he was forgiven his transgression and almost immediately became the Joint Master of the South Shropshire Hunt. He did come back to gliding some years later and in 1986 completed his Diamond 'C'. As he said "I think that was my last record—Gold 'C' in 1947, my Diamond in 1986. Will anyone take longer?"

It was agreed that Charles would fly first while we prepared the T.21 and took it to the launch point. He said that as soon as he saw the glider in position he would land and then fly with Doc. We did not see or hear from Charles again until noon when he telephoned from a farm at the bottom of the hill asking for a retrieve. The Cambridge boys immediately agreed to bring him back and, hooking a trailer on to their Beaverette retrieve vehicle being driven by David Martlew, set off down the very steep Asterton road on the west side of the hill. Half way down he jack-knifed with the Beaverette fortuitously burying its nose in the hill. Unperturbed by this set-back, one of their number ran back up the hill and proceeded to back their other retrieve vehicle, a modified Ambulance, down the hill. Then in true Cambridge style they decided to modify the trailer so that they could tow it backwards up the hill.

In the meantime we had rushed down in the Jowett van and soon realised that a classic major Cambridge re-build was about to start and there was nothing we could do to speed things up. As Doc Cotton wanted Charles back on top in order to fly, Ron Macfie and I jumped into Charles Wingfield's very grand limo and went in search of his trailer. As soon as we had found it and hooked up we set off going the long way down the hill taking the Ratlinghope (pronounced 'Ratchup' by the locals) road. When we arrived at the farm Charles told us sadly that we had not brought his trailer but being ever resourceful Redhillites we suggested that one Olympia trailer was just as good as another until we looked inside and saw that there was already a glider in there.

"No problem" we said and pressed on back to the Mynd to get the correct empty trailer. Half way up Ratchup we ran out of petrol. The Cambridge Club had blocked Asterton, we now blocked the other road so all the routes up to the top from the west were now impassable. I quite enjoyed the nice long walk back to the site to find a can of petrol and eventually we returned triumphantly to Charles who by this time was being entertained to dinner by two charming ladies in the farmhouse. On hearing what had happened he casually mentioned that we should have looked in the boot as he always carried a gallon of petrol just in case! It was on the stroke of midnight when we arrived back at the club complete with Charles, his car, glider and trailer. The Cambridge Club entourage beat us back by thirty minutes.

That week we doubled the cross country miles ever flown from the site and were highly amused when at the week-end some staid Midlanders said how sorry they were that the west wind had not blown for us. On hearing about the wonderful thermals one replied "Damn nuisance aren't they!" Since it was a ridge site, the term 'hillbound' was certainly apposite and had a negative effect on some of their pilots.

After the Mynd we visited a small club operating at Staverton airfield between Cheltenham and Gloucester. When we found that no launches were possible because their cable retrieve vehicle had broken down we offered to pull the cable out by hand and five of us started on the task. Half way back to the launch point, the cable broke. The visit was not a total failure as each of us had an aero-tow in Toby Fisher's Olympia, a charming man who was Kitty Wills's brother.

On one non-flying day we decided that we ought to visit Tewkesbury Abbey for a bit of culture to be followed by a trip on the river. John Edwards, now an eminent doctor and a Fellow of the Royal Society, then a veritable pillar of the Cambridge Club came with us. A great character, but what we did not know was that apart from rolling off the hangar roof he was allegedly very accident prone. As we drank in the atmosphere and history of the Abbey someone pointed up at the battle honour flags hanging from the wall dating back to Waterloo and earlier. Just as John pointed out a really old relic which was little more than a few tatters of material attached to a pole, the whole thing fell off the wall. Later that day with Ann Douglas (Welch) driving the boat we had hired, and just as we had persuaded her to ignore the instructions and see how fast we could go, John sitting at the back spotted an interesting cable. Being a small boy at heart he pulled it for all he was worth, the rudder turned through ninety degrees and we promptly rammed the bank. At a pub we made him drink two pints of strong Gloucestershire scrumpy for every one of ours and thus ensured that he was in no state to cause any more mayhem on the return journey.

At their Bourn airfield site near Cambridge they used their Kranich two seater to show pupils the joys of gliding but solo training was carried out flying the Slingsby Cadet. One day a pupil wanted to practise a stall on his own having been shown what it was like in the Kranich. On that occasion his Instructor Gordon Bell had prevented excessive stick movements as his pupil was a highly trained athlete capable of great strength and endurance. "Pull the stick back until the glider stalls and then push it forward until you pick up speed. When you feel back pressure on the stick, level off" was the instruction given before take-off. Up went the Cadet, then came the stall but when the unsuspecting pupil pushed the stick forward he found that it went down almost to the cockpit floor as the wooden stop was missing. By then he was flying upside down but with great presence of mind, he managed to grab the stick again and proceeded to pull it back for all he was worth followed by a normal landing. Ted Warner, the resident Cambridge Ground Engineer, watching this extraordinary manoeuvre fell over backwards in his excitement.

Gilroy 'Gil' Phillips, a mighty man, still 'Mine Host' at the Clarence House Hotel in Tenby West Wales and even more grandly erstwhile Mayor of that sleepy seaside resort sent me his account of a typical Club happening. He writes: "To try something different a few of us agreed that we would do a 180 degree turn immediately on release at a launch height of about 800/900 feet, fly fast down the runway and pull up over the launch point while someone timed us with a stop watch. My own flight in the Slingsby Tutor went according to plan until I did a sharp pull-up over the launch point at something under three hundred feet. It was said to be nearly vertical and the 'deadly hush' came far quicker than my reactions. I instinctively gripped the controls firmly to stop the clutching hand from winning and my dinghy sailing experience said 'sternway in irons' so I 'up helmed' and pulled the stick hard back. The tail immediately flicked up over my head and the horizon appeared in its normal position, just above the nose, but with the ground uppermost. As dried mud and one small spanner flew into my face, I looked 'up' to see a clutch of pale pink round faces looking 'down' at me hanging hard in my straps. There was nothing else to do except sit there with the stick hard back in my stomach and wait. The Tutor dived and levelled off at high speed crossing the boundary hedge downwind at under fifty feet.

Because of the difficulty of de-rigging a Tutor with all those struts, turnbuckles and flying wires, it was not done to land outside the airfield. In any case I did not think that I could stop in the field as my speed was too high. I then did what turned out to be my first chandelle and found myself approaching the main road at hedge top height. I had a blurred impression of a line of cars running on to the grass verge and stopping, after which I floated gently up the runway, losing speed until after a normal main wheel and tailskid touchdown, the front main skid grounded at the feet of our Chief Flying Instructor Paul Blanchard. I sat quite still watching him, complete with his green Tyrolean hat on his head, walk slowly round the Tutor eventually arriving at the cockpit. Solemnly he presented me with a small part of a bush which he had removed from the tailskid and said "You are a very lucky fellow, please do not do that again"."

Gil's spirited rendition of the famous Victorian dirge was *de rigeur* at every Cambridge Club gathering:

"Oh, the wheel came off the hearse
The coffin fell out on the road
The driver got out and said with a shout
Well, I'm blowed!
The widow got down to the driver
In a mournful voice she said
Oh what has my husband down to you
That you muck him about when he's dead."

The Cambridge Club members were very proud of their light blue coloured Olympia. Had it been a wartime Lancaster bomber they might have painted bombs on the side of the fuselage to show how many missions it had flown. This Glider should have had 'A', 'B', 'C', Silver 'C', 'North Sea' and 'Irish Sea' painted on the fuselage.

First Jimmy Grantham on a cross-country found himself out over the North Sea. No one would ever believe my account of this fabulous story so the gallant pilot offered to write it himself:

"The date was 25 April 1950. The original rather ambitious plan was to try and reach Dover and see if conditions were right for a Channel crossing. This intention was frustrated in the end by a radical shift in wind direction from the forecast North Westerly to a little south of west together with a big increase in wind strength. After an autotow at Bourn I went straight to cloud base and subsequent climbs took me up to 8,500 feet in cloud. I started the final climb over West Mersea in very strong lift, went into cloud at 6,000 feet and then climbed steadily to nearly 14,000 feet flying blind the whole way. Fumbling with the oxygen which I had never used before did not help my concentration much and wearing the mask caused my glasses to mist up! When it was obvious I had reached the top, I first set a South Westerly course still in cloud hoping to compensate for the crosswind drift but when a brief emergence from cloud at 9,000 feet showed nothing but sea below I changed course to due West. All this time the Air Speed Indicator was inoperative and the wings and canopy were heavily iced up so the rate of sink was horrendous. Emerging below cloud at 5,000 feet the coast was only dimly discernible a long way ahead, there was still ice on the wings and it soon became obvious we would not make it. I looked around for ships to land near and be rescued but saw none and went ahead to touch down as near to the shore as possible.

The actual ditching went very well. I kept the tail well down to avoid nose-diving underwater and we settled onto the sea in a cloud of spray over a mile offshore three miles north of Walton-on-the-Naze. The sea being relatively calm, the Olympia floated well but the cockpit soon began to fill up from below. Having quickly removed the canopy, I hung onto it using it to help me balance after I had climbed onto and then stood up on the centre section which was awash after the Olympia had fully settled down in the water. This position had two advantages, only my lower legs got wet and I was much better able to see and be seen. I signalled frantically at people I could see on the distant beach.

Later I learnt that someone saw this but thought I was waving a friendly greeting from a boat! After half- an-hour I was getting really apprehensive and thinking of trying to swim ashore. Wisely I resisted this impulse—the sea was very cold and I had no idea of the tidal currents. No one had observed the 'landing'. I was told later that luckily the Coast Guard at Walton were keeping a good lookout and eventually spotted the floating wreckage. The first I knew of this was when the maroon went up exploding with a loud bang to call out the lifeboat. Then came the message flashed in Morse code by Aldis lamp "Help is coming". You can imagine my feeling of relief, all I had to do now was to hang on until the lifeboat arrived which it did some thirty minutes later. To my annoyance however the coxswain stood off about thirty feet, threw me a lifebelt on the end of a rope and told me to jump in and grab hold of it. I protested that I had stayed dry so far and if he came alongside I could climb on board without getting wet—but he refused. I later discovered that he thought the Olympia was a powered aircraft and he was afraid that he would damage the lifeboat's hull on a submerged propeller or engine.

No sooner was I on board the lifeboat, terribly relieved and grateful but soaked to the skin and colder and more uncomfortable than I had been for the previous hour on the Olympia wing, than a Royal Air Force rescue launch from Felixstowe arrived having heard the news on the radio. They were most peeved at being beaten by the Walton men. Their doctor insisted on coming on board to examine me before they left. We then set about trying to tow the Olympia back to Walton. For the first two attempts we used a grappling iron which soon came off and incidentally was not doing the glider much good. The only satisfactory method in my opinion was to pass a rope around the mainspar. As none of the crew really knew what was required I did the job myself getting wet again up to the waist in the process. Also the nose of the glider got bashed to pieces by the lifeboat's hull when we went alongside. The tow was a slow business since at any speed of more than two knots the Olympia disappeared under water with only the tip of the fin showing and the strain must have been tremendous.

In the meantime the crew radioed ashore so that my people could be told what had happened. They also gave me dry clothes many sizes too big but better still, the biggest mug of rum I have ever seen. By the time we reached Walton pier I was in a very happy state and assisted in hauling the Olympia up on to the beach through the surf. This was the third time I got wet that afternoon . Then the local policeman turned up and wanted to take a statement from me so having rescued the barograph we went to the police station where I proceeded to dry the chart and myself in front of a roaring fire while telling my story. In return he gave me a certificate that said the barograph had been opened in his presence so that I could claim Gold 'C' height! I was then handed over to the local Shipwrecked Seamen's Aid Society who kindly supplied a complete change of clothing, a room in a hotel and a hot bath. To cap it all just before getting into the bath the Press arrived and I had to give an interview in my underpants. I remember one of the headlines to the story was "Glider pilot plunges 13,000 feet into North Sea"."

When the sky blue Olympia had been thoroughly dried out and repaired the Club decided to visit Bill Crease's mountain site at Clwyd Gate in North Wales. Near his restaurant Bill had carved out a launch run for the bungey team with the ropes running through the chicken run. Being an adventurous lot they explored various other possible launching sites in the area and one day went to the Great Orme's Head near Llandudno where they found a good bungey site and an adequate field for landing back on top of the cliff. Several pilots had very good flights including Mike Gee who described his as "one of my star flights ever, particularly as half way up the cliff face was a road and each time a bus passed along it I would dive down and fly alongside the bus and then climb up again above the cliff". The next time they visited that site the wind was from a different direction and they drew lots to see who would fly first. Mike was the lucky one or so they said at the time! His story too has to be told in the first person and this is what he wrote:

"Shortly after the launch I turned left, away from our landing field but this proved to be a mistake as there was not any lift. So I turned the other way and there was none there either. By now I was losing height and realised that not only would I not reach the field but I might not even reach the shore. The promenade was fairly empty and I thought of landing there but even that proved too far. Then I saw the lifeboat launching slipway—it was a bit short and with my luck I would probably meet the lifeboat coming down as I went up—but even that proved to be unreachable. The sea it was and just as I expected to hear the skid rustling through the top of the water there was a dirty great bang and suddenly I was completely submerged. In about two seconds flat I was out of my parachute harness and sitting on top of the centre section waiting anxiously until a little man in a rowing boat came and rescued me. That was not one of my star flights, it only lasted four minutes!"

On another flight some years later he was struck by lightning but did not jump out. He is very proud of his 'Goldfish' badge. If you jump in earnest using an Irvin parachute, you are made a member of the Caterpillar Club, if you land in the sea you become a member of the Goldfish Club—a rare honour for glider pilots, though trust the Cambridge University Gliding Club to have two!

One other story among many concerning the Cantab Mob was the occasion when they were retrieving a glider with their Beaverette. This type of comparatively cheap mode of transport, fitted with a Standard 40 engine was much favoured by gliding clubs. Jack Rice of 'Rice Trailers' fame realised that this light armoured car could easily be adapted for civilian gliding use, was cheap and easy to buy in war surplus equipment sales. Jack had come across these strange fighting vehicles during the last year of the war when the Air Training Corps used them extensively for their gliding schools. Denis Dawson now takes up the story of how they bought the first batch:

"We chose the Tipsy aircraft to fly from our base at Rearsby airfield to the place near Uffingham where the auction was going to take place. Jack did two or three passes at a hundred feet while I looked at the Beaverettes lined up below. He then ordered me to fly at no more than fifty feet so that he could have a really close view and select the ones he considered the cleanest! We arrived at the auction and managed to buy six or eight of the ones we wanted for an average price of £35.00. These were driven, sometimes on Jack Rice's trade plates, to his Trailer factory at Crosby near Leicester where the gun turret and most of the thick armoured plating were removed".

The other clubs soon latched on to them and used them mainly for cable towing. Visualise the scene. The Cambridge crew towing a trailer on the King's highway when a cyclist got tangled up between the Beaverette and trailer. They stopped, picked her up, found she was unhurt, dusted her down and sent her on her way. Fearing the strength and displeasure of 'the Law' and, in truth, in case someone had witnessed the mishap, they decided to report the incident at the nearest police station. "I wish to inspect your vehicle and with this here accelerometer which I will clamp to said vehicle I will test your brakes" said the Inspector. Good as his word, the device was attached, the policeman perched on the Beaverette and off they drove. "Stop" shouted our man and the accelerometer promptly flew off and smashed on the road in front. Back to the cop shop they went to get a new one. While the Inspector and Ken Machin were inside searching for a spare, Laurie Vandome with great foresight decided to tighten the brake cables just to make certain that they passed the test. Back came Ken, the Law and a replacement instrument. Again off they went except this time there were three new factors in play. First the policeman told Ken to drive faster, second he had decided to stand up holding on to the steel plate in front of him with one hand while clutching his precious piece of high tech in the other and last, but by no means least, Ken did not know what Laurie had done to the brakes. When the order "Stop" was given, the new accelerometer and the policeman flew through the air with the greatest of ease and damaged His Majesty's property, i.e. the tarmac road surface. When they got back to the Station, the Sergeant on duty said "You haven't broken another one, have you?" to which the classic reply was "Yes, and can we have another policeman as well?".

The Surrey members liked visiting Cambridge especially for the annual dinner at which the Inter-University Brunt Trophy was awarded. The Dinner held at the Dorothy Café in the centre of town was, by our standards, a very staid and proper affair and so we decided to liven things up.

John Pringle, the President of the Cambridge University Gliding Club presided in grand style. During the war he had made a major contribution to the development of radar before returning to his academic life at Cambridge after the war, finally ending up at Oxford University as Professor of Zoology. On this occasion Professor Sir David Brunt, who was not only an eminent meteorologist but also a Vice President of the British Gliding Association, was to award the prize himself.

First we tied our linen napkins together and passed them up the table with instructions for each person to attach his own. When the sausage reached John Pringle just as he was introducing the great man, he calmly added his own napkin and moved it on past the guest of honour without a murmur. We felt quite cheated, but after all John had been a very active glider pilot himself for years and knew how to deflate people like us. At our end of the table there was a stupendous bowl of flowers and we wondered whether that would be more appropriate.

Up it went and reached Sir David just as he got up to make his speech. Quite unconcerned he looked at it for a while, said "Nice, isn't it" and passed it on. After that we behaved immaculately and realised that at last we had met our match.

Hauling the Olympia up onto the beach

Chapter 6

Comps and all

Bloody Competitions
Words by Pat Wood

These comps are just a bloody cuss
They go from bad to bloody wuss
And no-one cares for bloody us
Bloody Competitions

The bloody weather's bloody bad
The bloody met man's bloody mad
No wonder we look bloody sad
Bloody Competitions

No bloody luck, no bloody skill
We're hardly on the bloody hill
Before we're feeling bloody ill
Bloody Competitions

The bloody flights are bloody fraught
Fraughter than they bloody ought
And when they're not they're bloody short
Bloody Competitions

Retrieves are awful bloody trials
We drive the trailers bloody miles
And all we get is bloody piles
Bloody Competitions

Best bloody place is bloody bed
With bloody ice on bloody head
Before we all drop bloody dead
Bloody Competitions

In August 1949 we entered the Surrey Weihe in the National Championships to be held at Camphill, the home of the Derby & Lancs Gliding Club. As we came from a beautifully maintained flat grass airfield, Camphill presented quite a challenge. Then an uneven, small boulder-strewn fairly narrow hilltop site, it was not the relatively smooth field we see to-day. It even had dry stream beds, when the rains came they caught out unsuspecting glider pilots as Tony Deane-Drummond discovered before the war when the tent which he had erected late one evening was washed away during the night. The site had a typical Derbyshire dry stone wall running along the edge of the field behind which, if the wind was blowing from the west on to the hill, there lurked a fearsome clutching hand.

As we approached Camphill by road we noticed with some alarm the small size of the surrounding fields which were inevitably enclosed by yet more dry stone walls. In Surrey Club parlance these were classic 'claptraps'. Walter Morison is credited with this descriptive expression for a field surrounded by obstructions which is too small to land in—but you just have! His other invention was 'The Fumble Factor' defined as the number of loose bits of the glider and trailer which can be forgotten and left behind in the field by the pilot and crew after an out-landing.

We soon discovered, when anyone was unlucky enough to damage one of these structures (not a recommended practice with a wooden glider which invariably came off worse in the encounter) rebuilding them was an art form which is handed down from father to son going back to Roman times. The uninitiated soon found that even very careful stone selection and placing was no guarantee of success and, just when you thought you had finished, the whole lot fell down and you had to start all over again.

The Camphill Crawl
Tune: 'Lambeth Walk'

Any time you're Camphill Way
Any evening, any day
You'll find us all, doing the Camphill Crawl
Every little road and drain
Helps to clear the snow and rain
And you'll find 'em all built from an old stone wall
Everyone's good and matey

Cause boulders with muck are weighty
"Why don't you clear the mud there?"
"Hi, there!"
"Dig there!"
Once you get in Basil's squad
Through the stones and mud you plod
You'll find us all doing the Camphill Crawl
Hey!

John Neilan, a British European Airways Captain; Derek Reid, the highly competent meteorologist who later emigrated to Australia and was a very active member of the Australian gliding scene and I were sharing the flying. We were up against stiff competition as not only were Philip Wills and Prince Birabongse of Siam also flying Weihes but also my old friends from RAF Germany were bringing three with them. In the event we came second and brought home the Du Garde Peach Trophy awarded to the best club team and £10 as well as the second prize of £20. Unheard of wealth for the Surrey Club.

The sweetheart of the Champs was a very fetching blonde called Margaret Swale who was flying her father's Olympia. Every day she wore a different trouser suit which looked for all the world like pyjamas and certainly helped to lift morale more than somewhat. It is said that King George V only ever gave his son Edward one tip on kingship: "Empty your bladder whenever you can". The last thing a competition pilot had to do prior to launching was to expel all surplus body fluid as built-in pee tubes were not yet fashionable in glider design. With the ever present Margaret this was difficult but Jerry Smith the local Chief Instructor came to our rescue. "What you do is sit on the ground, spread your legs, cover yourself with an air map and Hey Presto!". He then proceeded to demonstrate just as La Swale rushed up shouting "You have pinched my map" and pulled it away. Entertainment factor high, success rate low so it was a case of back to the drawing board.

What is interesting about the 1949 Comps is that out of the thirty gliders, only five were not team entries. It was not the rich man's sport as are present day competitions. The programme reads like a race meeting at Goodwood or Ascot to-day. We had a Clerk of the Course, an Assistant Clerk, three Judges, three Chief Marshals, Starters and three Royal Aero Club Stewards, all frightfully socially OK pillars of the aviation community. But nevertheless it was fun.

Because of the adjacent small fields and the prevailing westerly winds, tasks in subsequent comps held at the site were set of the 'down wind dash' variety which always came to an abrupt end when the east coast of England was reached. When the 1954 World Championships were held there, the site acquired a new name, 'Damphill' since that is what the foreigners called it because it rained so much.

For me one flight came to an extremely abrupt end when, due to sheer carelessness, I had to land downwind into a cornfield on the very edge of a steep cliff right on the coast. The tailplane and the corn had a bit of a fight, the corn won and I was out for the rest of the Comps. Out of dark clouds, however, sometimes emerge silver linings! I had persuaded a cigarette manufacturer—by coincidence the producer of the 'Nasties' we were given free at the end of the war—to pay me £50 to put advertising posters on either side of the Weihe trailer.. When the Comps Officials asked to borrow my trailer as a crowd barrier, I readily agreed. The Tobacco Company's biggest customer was driving through the Peak District when to his astonishment he saw a Cigarette Poster. Knowing that it was strictly against the law to put up any advertising hoardings of any sort in this National Park, he was somewhat puzzled. On his return to his office, he telephoned the Sales Director and congratulated him on their remarkable feat. When Rothmans checked they were so pleased that they doubled their payment to me—which paid for the repair.

For the rest of those Comps, whenever I appeared at briefing, my 'friends' sang "How much is that Weihe in the window, the one with the waggly tail?" After the Comps, Peggy Mieville 'sold' the sides of all the Dunstable trailers to Ovaltine for £20 each per year which in my view was far too little. After some cars were 'carved up' by swinging glider trailers advertising the chocolate drink, the advertising value was deemed to be negative and the scheme was scrubbed. Pity really, it might have been developed into quite a little gold mine for gliding.

Pilots soon realised that rather than land at the goal airfield on the coast such as North Denes or Ingoldmell—whenever the latter was set, there was always a cry at the morning briefing of "Not Jingle Bells again!"—they could squeeze a few more distance points by landing on the beach just beyond the airfield boundary. This ploy gave rise to a famous story which has survived for the past thirty plus years though somewhat modified. It was alleged that John Williamson was the first to arrive to be confronted by a large irate policeman, possibly even the original Police Constable Plod, who accused John of endangering the Great British Public who were paddling about in the surf with their trouser legs rolled up. No amount of hand wringing apologies on John's part satisfied the man in blue and so he resorted to some gentle name dropping. "You can't arrest me, my father comes from these parts, he is Henry Williamson, the author of 'Tarka the Otter'". Just then Alf Warminger landed and when the policeman had a go at him, Alf said "You can't arrest me, I am the Sheriff of Norwich". Finally Peter Scott landed and when the law recognised him he asked him for an autograph and gave up the unequal struggle. It made a good story but it is time to relate what really occurred. It happened during a Dunstable Nationals. George Burton was the first to land and P.C.Plod had no trouble nailing him. When Chuck Bentson, Dan Smith and Geoffery Stephenson landed in quick succession he called for help and a very officious Police Inspector joined the fray. It was only when the Sheriff of Norwich and Peter Scott had joined the party and the Inspector had secured the latter's autograph were the pilots allowed to enlist the help of interested bystanders to pull the gliders up the beach before the tide came in.

The Bristol Song
Most likely written by Bill Gotch and Bill Wills.
Tune as 'Rule Britannia'

Now once there was a fellow who had an ambition to fly
So he did decide
He'd learn to glide
And get into the sky
But when he made enquiries where gliders could be found
They said they've got 'em
At Lulsgate Bottom
But mostly on the ground

Chorus:
Singing Rule Britannia, Britannia rules the sky
And Britons never never never shall be
Mar-ri-ed to the angels if they never never learn to fly

So off he went to Lulsgate to see what he could do
And there he met
The gliding set
A very motley crew
He asked them could they help him to get into the sky
And they all replied, if you want to glide
You must see the C.F.I.

Chorus—yet again

Then from a nearby hangar they dragged a curious thing
On a wheel it stood   Some bits of wood
Surmounted by a wing
On a perilous perch they placed him and said "Now do or die"
And with a shout   They cried "All out!"
And hurled him in the sky

Chorus again and again

He very soon discovered and quickly got the knack
It's all a trick
What you do with a stick
And how you pull it back
But if you push it forward, then down you go like a diver
With a sickening sound
You hit the ground
And it only costs you a fiver

More Chorus

So off he went to Roundway for soaring on the slope
With visions he
Of a Silver 'C'
His heart was full of hope
But all he found at Roundway was tears and sweat and blood
With piles of muck
And the vehicles stuck

In an endless sea of mud

Chorus for the last time

And now he is proficient a sailplane pilot wise
The soaring kind
With a sore behind
He sails the summer skies
And if you want a 'line-shoot' why he can tell the tale
Of the big Cu-nim
That swallowed him
Like Jonah and the Whale

In May the following year I visited the Bristol Gliding Club and flew some of their gliders at Lulsgate Bottom, now the Bristol International Airport. Some days before, their T.21 had landed in the middle of the airfield and the only other glider out that day was a Tutor being flown by an early solo pilot. It is hard to believe, but on landing, he managed to ram the two-seater from behind. It is quite extraordinary how often this seems to happen as some early solos do seem strangely attracted to other gliders when coming in to land.

Lorne Welch used to preach safe flying by explaining that the time taken to repair a small patch in the fabric takes the same time as the pilot retrieving his glider on his own without any mechanical aid from one end of the airfield, and a near write-off prang repair takes about as long as your man pulling a glider back on his own from Warsaw! It was a valuable lesson which we all took on board.

Above: Many hands make light work at 'Jingle Bells'

Right: Stamps from 17 countries—the UK is not one of them

Chapter 7

Denmark

The Danish Air Force had ordered three new Olympias from the manufacturer, Elliotts of Newbury. Horace Buckingham, the owner, decided that his test pilot would deliver them, being towed to Denmark behind the Elliott towing and touring aeroplane they had just completed. The tug pilot was to be a gentleman called appropriately Mr.Twogood. The test pilot should, for the record, remain nameless. He did, however, have a forceful personality and decided that he would have a telephone link from the glider to the tug so that he could give instructions to the pilot though not vice versa. Having cleared Customs at Lympne in Kent, they hooked up, both pilots climbed into their respective steeds and the tug pilot tried to start his engine. It would not start so he set the throttle, got out and swung the propeller by hand. The next bit is rather like the famous Hoffnung story about the Irish Bricklayer, the Bricks and the Bucket. The throttle was set open too much, the engine fired and the tug and glider combination started rolling. At this juncture the glider pilot with great presence of mind jumped out and ran towards the tug, presumably intending to climb in and cut the power. Unfortunately not only did he get tangled up in the tow rope but he had also forgotten to pull the cable release in the glider. He did manage to get clear of the rope and watched the tug and glider proceed across the airfield until both were wrecked when they hit first the far hedge and then rolled into a ditch.

The Cavalry in the shape of the Surrey Club came to the rescue and we were awarded the contract to deliver the other two Olympias. David Ince was towed by Lorne Welch in the first one which had been left on an airfield in Belgium and on his return I was the pilot for the second glider. On 5 June 1950, before leaving Redhill, Lorne warned me that he might fall asleep in the Auster tug and if I saw his head in an unusual position I was to pull his tail to wake him up! The first leg from Redhill to Lympne took fifty minutes. From there straight out to sea climbing to three thousand in the middle of the Channel whereupon Lorne started descending so that we crossed the French coast very low. All I remember about the sea crossing is that I spent my time looking for ships just in case the rope decided to part or the ring pull out of the nose Ottfur hook. I was not really a very happy bunny, water is all right in small quantities in whisky but not when it is below you in large dollops. We reached Eelde in Holland after three hours and fifty-five minutes flying and I was so pleased at the thought of landing that I aerobated all the way down only to find that the barograph locker door had opened and inside we had stored all our papers, money and passports. Luckily nothing had fallen out so that my hastily carefully prepared speech to Lorne proved unnecessary.

"I might fall asleep over the Zuider Zee" said Lorne. And he did! Gently swaying from side to side woke him up much to my relief. The leg to Belringe on the west coast of Denmark took just two hours and fifty minutes. The last leg from there to Varlose, the military airfield at Copenhagen, which lasted seventy minutes was pure magic. We flew no higher than five hundred feet and every time Lorne saw a fairyland castle he would circle round it and then move on.

A Danish Air Force colonel welcomed us on arrival and detailed a Major to show us to our quarters. After eight and three quarters hours on tow my priority was a large drink and a bath. Imagine our surprise when we were taken to the station hospital and two dishy nurses showed us to our rooms. They are no fools these Danes. They knew! That night after a splendid dinner and ample liquid refreshment in the mess the Colonel decided to take us out to Tivoli Gardens, the Copenhagen pleasure park which caters for all needs. I do not remember too much about that night other than the two Spanish potato salesmen who joined the party quite early on. Why they adopted us or indeed who they were I never discovered. But boy, was I grateful the next morning when I woke up in my hospital bed; the services of the doctors and nurses were most welcome and very necessary. The next day the Danes invited us to fly up to Karup, an airfield in the north of the country and a day later we flew back to Redhill. Trips like that only come once in a lifetime and if ever you get the chance do not hesitate to take it.

The following month Jack Karran and I, both flying Olympias, managed to break the United Kingdom Out and Return record flying from Redhill to Netheravon and back. Jack was something terribly grand in the Ministry of Civil Aviation and one of his stories is worth repeating over and over again. Every gliding club occasionally has an outbreak of low unauthorised aerobatics performed by pilots showing off near the ground. When this happened at Redhill, in his quiet way of speaking Jack said "During the war I was instructing at a RAF Flying Training School in Rhodesia and we suffered from this problem. I asked the Air Ministry to send out two psychiatrists to investigate this phenomenon. When they had completed their task we asked them to announce the result of their findings in front of all the pilots. They announced that their research showed without doubt that anyone who carried out unauthorised low aerobatics invariably suffered from an unsatisfactory sex life. "Do you know," said Jack, "that stopped it overnight".

At a seminar of British Sporting World Champions we found that the common thread which they all shared was an almost ruthless determination to win, to fully understand the rules and know how to bend them without falling foul of the officials. Philip Wills was no exception and during the Championships at Camphill he perfected his art of supreme 'one-upmanship'. Very much in keeping with the image of the Great Man, he always wore spats when he flew and just as modern professional footballers seem to feign injury during a match for tactical reasons, Philip used his spats in much the same way. Launching was on to the hill by means of a short winch run and when your turn came off you went. Not Philip—when his turn came to be launched he would suddenly find that his spats needed adjusting which would miraculously be completed just as a good-looking cumulus cloud drifted towards the hill face. Dear Philip—he had a similar trick which he practised at BGA Council meetings. When things were not going his way, he developed a ploy which transfixed new members but which the more experienced of us knew meant that he was about to hoist the red flag similar to those flown at ranges when firing is in progress. He would start a sentence, stop, produce a large sheet of special paper, tear off a small square, pack some tobacco into it, push it into his pipe, light it and then produce a vast cloud of smoke. By now the poor unfortunates would have lost all concentration and Philip, ever the picador, was ready for the kill.

We also learnt something new. Quite a lot of us were milling around in the duty thermal over the site when suddenly we were surrounded by streams of lavatory paper. Now we are all used to meeting birds, straw, aeroplanes and other gliders in the air but never loo paper. The answer it transpired was that dear Wing Commander Sandy Sanders, a RAF pilot, had invented his own thermal indicator. By throwing out streams of paper he reckoned he would see where the core of the thermal was and follow this paper chain upwards. As we all know, the Air Navigation Order states that only water or finely divided sand may be thrown out of flying machines without the prior permission of the Minister! Sandy's ploy did not work but merely goes to prove that glider pilots must be a tiny bit mad.

The only magazine devoted to gliding at that time was *Sailplane and Glider.* The first issue was on 6th September 1930 and the cover price for the then weekly was just three pennies in old money. It is interesting to note that this was the period of intense interest in our sport with very many clubs being formed all over the country though the depression year of 1931 sadly finished most of them off. By 1948 with a cover price six times higher and now only appearing as a monthly, the Editor was a very strange human being indeed. He invented and nurtured a vendetta against Philip Wills, the British Gliding Association and the Surrey Club which we regarded as a total joke although it meant that he never mentioned any of them in his self styled 'The first Journal devoted to Soaring and Gliding'. The man was really a Mark I buffoon and we all tried to think of ways to cut him down to size but it was Lawrence Wright of the London Club who dreamt up the best joke to play on him.

A letter from someone called R.K.Hafid posted in Cairo, Egypt, was sent to the Editor giving a full report of a lecture given by Professor Aziz to the *'Societé des Planeurs de l'Université et du Cité du Caire'* describing his pioneering research into the Pyramid cloud, the Arabic name was translated as 'The Umbrella of Khufu', a phenomenon which had been seen by travellers ever since the Pyramids were built. He described how the students at the University had adapted a war surplus Waco fifteen place military glider and as a result had achieved startling performance figures of best L/D at the speed of 64.5kph, a stalling speed of 55kph and a minimum sink rate of 1.2 metres per second. With this fine machine, the Professor was able to prove that the cloud was in reality a Pyramid induced standing wave in which Aziz and the Chief Instructor were able to climb to the base of the cloud at 2265 metres. At this point Aziz 'became ill' and had to abandon the flight. In the course of landing the glider was damaged and so no further research was possible. However, the Professor cordially invited glider pilots from England and other countries to bring their sailplanes to Egypt and sample his wave in order to gain their Gold 'C' height. This splendid spoof complete with some remarkable photographs, one of which had pride of place on the cover, duly appeared in the May 1948 issue of 'S & G' and the only person who believed every word was the Editor.

By the beginning of 1950 it was decided that the British Gliding Association should publish its own magazine and so *Gliding* was born. Under the editorship of Jacques Cocheme and later the great Doctor (Doc) A.E.Slater of penny whistle fame it very quickly gained a large readership. Just at the time when the Editor of *Sailplane and Glider* incurred the wrath of the Inland Revenue and Her Majesty's Commissioners of Customs and Excise and was sentenced to serve a term as a 'guest' of Her Majesty.

I was able to persuade the owner of the magazine to give it to the BGA and thus in that year we combined the two under the title of *Sailplane and Gliding*. You can well imagine that the Council spent many happy hours arguing long and hard over the title as the word 'Sailplane' was not in common usage in Britain though our American cousins had adopted it some years before. In the February 1958 issue of 'S & G' our Editor wrote that the word had been invented by Sir George Cayley to describe his first model glider in 1804. Now, nearly two hundred years later, we tend to describe training machines as 'gliders' and the sleek high performance soaring beauties as 'sailplanes', so honour is satisfied.

Margaret Kahn's award winning oil painting, now a coloured limited edition print

Chapter 8

The BGA Ball

In December 1950, the British Gliding Association celebrated its twenty-first birthday and we resolved to mark it in style. At that time the noble Lord Londonderry had allowed us and the other sporting aviation organisations to use his fabulous mansion in London's Park Lane as our headquarters. It was a most impressive building, full of Roman and Grecian statues, beautiful paintings and the most imposing staircase which led to our offices off the central ballroom. It was exactly the right setting for a 'Gliding Ball'. The assembled company was knee-deep in celebrities and much to 'the Gaffer's' surprise, everyone behaved beautifully and he announced that other Balls would be held in the future. In 1953 to celebrate Philip Wills winning the World Championships in Spain the previous year, we organised another grand affair. The terribly socially OK magazine, *The Tatler,* much read by the Upper Crust and members of the Café Society, sent their Social Editor complete with a photographer to record the proceedings. One of the photographs which appeared the following week was a picture of 'Mr. Ray Brigden deep in conversation with Miss Brenda Horsfield enjoying an aperitif before dancing'. It was almost certainly the first time that *The Tatler* had printed a photograph of someone holding a pint of beer! My Committee members had decorated the venue with great style but Philip Wills' wife Kitty decided that the large naked marble statues of males might offend the sensibilities of the young and so rushed round sticking paper bunches of grapes over certain parts of the male statues.

It was a great success and we decided to hold a ball the following year. On that occasion John Profumo, certainly the best and most effective Parliamentary Under Secretary at the Ministry of Civil Aviation to look after our interests, the junior Minister in the Department which controlled our destiny, came as our Guest of Honour with his lovely actress wife Valerie Hobson. The Cambridge Club fielded Lionel Alexander as part of the entertainment. Old men do forget and when checking the facts with him in 1982 Lionel wrote "unfortunately the script is not in my scrap-book. I call to mind that the original was delivered on bits of paper and in pencil. It was typed as well, but I am fairly sure that P... W... impounded the only copy.

We shall never know. However, this is a textually corrupt transcript of a longhand note of the speech delivered by 'Mister John Profundis M.P., the Parliamentary Under-Secretary of the Ministry of Fag and Disheries at the British Gliding Association annual reception held at Londonderry House.

" My friends, for you are my friends, all of you even though I have never met most of you before and, with any luck, will never see you again, my Minister the Secretary of State has asked me to make profuse apologies on his behalf because, greatly to his regret and in all sincerity, he has been unavoidably detained by a subsequent engagement. My friends, I bring you good news. For many years, your tireless representatives have bent the Ministerial ears of my predecessors, in the hope, not of any financial hand-out (which, given the potential expenditure of billions and the certainty of ultimate bankruptcy which would undoubtedly have been forthcoming) but of intangible assistance with regard to access to disused airfields. I do not doubt that, in aiming at this mark, they failed to appreciate the enormity of what they proposed. To accede to them, I must tell you, would be to shake the Constitution to its foundation garments, by breaching the '30 year' rule. You have not heard of this rule? Let me then explain that it is enshrined in the mists of constitutional convention so that, unlike statute law, it means what I say it means. It establishes the principle that, once the RAF have abandoned an airfield, which moment is defined as 21 years after the death of the last resident night-watchman, then 30 years must elapse before the airfield may be used by or sold to anyone other than an influential property developer.

My friends, this pillar of the Constitution notwithstanding, the representations to which I have referred have not fallen on deaf ears, however bent. On the contrary, my Secretary of State has authorised me to say, and I add my personal and independent confirmation that the policy of Her Majesty's government is henceforth and until the times do alter to undertake to provide to the British gliding movement every assistance in its power —short of action.

My friends, it is the view of all of us in government that you have richly deserved this new policy. Among the Goliaths of the great aviation vested interests, the gliding David, independent, determined, self-regulating, stands with its finger in the dyke holding back the tide of legislation that threatens to engulf it in the burning deck of the statute book. That is why we have set up an independent body (soon to be announced) with power to make regulations designed to redress the balance between David and Goliath, by outlawing the use of David's sling. In this way (so the members-designate of this new body assure me) will the rule of law in the air, with justice for all, be established.

My friends, happy is the man (and, of course, the statutory woman) who partakes of ambrosia, the food of the Gods, in the shape of this, the purest form of flight, the inheritance of Icarus. I see around me healthy, smiling faces. I sense by your loud laughter during my little speech your high spirits and well-being. It is accordingly clear to me that mastery of your strange machines holds no terror for you. As the man who, for the political moment, controls your destinies, this gives me confidence in your practical abilities. As for theory, I have gained, by talking to your Chairman, a new insight into the principles of soaring flight which will enable me better to discharge my duties on your behalf. It will of course be the Chairman's turn to speak next. When he does, perhaps he could find a moment to answer one question that still perplexes me—what do you do when the wind drops?.

The time, my friends, has come to thank you, on my own behalf and that of my absent Secretary of State, for entertaining me. As I have already hinted, we in the Ministry have great plans for you. In the future, when plans have come to fruition, look back I beg you to this occasion and remember that it was I who suggested to you your slogan for to-day, which is "You never had it so good" ".

All of us, especially John Profumo enjoyed this tremendously except 'The Gaffer', Philip Wills, who did not look at all certain whether a Ministerial leg-pull was wise. Knowing that he of all people was adept at fighting officialdom and was doing so to great effect on our behalf we decided that perhaps he was showing solidarity with his fellow Old Harrovian and just hereditary good manners which dictates that you must never insult a guest even if the satirist was also an O.H. as indeed Lionel Alexander is. Nevertheless, it was a brilliant satire and I am only sorry that the full text does not exist to-day though maybe one day one of his sons might find it among P...W...'s papers.

Some years later when we were head to head over the protracted battle for Lasham with countless Ministers, Under-Secretaries and so called Civil Servants who invariably finished off their letters with 'I have the honour to be Sir, Your obedient Servant' we were subjected to this form of official 'gobbledegook' for real and they could not understand why we had wry smiles when they started on their diatribes.

In fact Lionel Alexander need not have composed his splendid spoof had he known of the letter sent by Lord Nathan, the Minister of Civil Aviation in November 1947 which was published in the Surrey and Imperial Club Year Book 1947/48. Three paragraphs are pure 'Profundis':

"The gliding clubs are at this time labouring under many difficulties, and the fact that they have achieved so much in this year is a great tribute to the energy, enthusiasm and public spirit of everyone concerned. I look forward to more plentiful times when this fine spirit will reap a greater reward.

I take a great interest in the gliding movement. However I cannot promise, in the present difficult condition of the country, that subsidies or supplies of material can be provided. So far as it is possible for us to do so, I and my Ministry will give all the assistance we can. Since I paid a visit to the National Competitions last June, and was able to make two brief flights as a passenger, I have been anxious to see more of the gliding clubs. I have been closely tied to my desk, but nevertheless have several times been ready to make such visits. But the weather is no kinder to Ministers than to club members and each time it has let me down. I hope for better in the future".

It really is an absolute classic which makes one wonder if there a school somewhere to which budding politicians are sent to learn 'double speak'.

Chapter 9

More of them and us

The London Gliding Club at Dunstable and us Surrey Redhillites kept up a splendid rivalry. We regarded them as a hill-bound crowd who with a few exceptions did not seem to relish or copy our cross-country activities. In truth they rather regarded us as a lot of noisy, big-headed yahoos which was probably fully justified but we felt it was time to teach them a few lessons. When the west wind blew directly on to their hill which allowed them to stooge up and down to their hearts content, they were not the earliest risers in the world. Knowing that hill soaring was possible all day, warm beds held a great attraction for them on cold winter's mornings. For safety reasons they restricted the number of gliders on their hill at any one time so we resolved to tow all our gliders over to their hill at first light and watch their reaction when they saw what we had done. After due consideration, in other words when Lorne Welch stopped us in our tracks, we had to dream up another scheme.

Word reached us that they had organised a fancy dress party so over we went all wearing Dinner Jackets. On our arrival we found the locals in a terrible state as they had invited a gang of nurses from the local hospital but had failed to lay on any transport. We immediately set off for them in the Surrey Club retrieve vehicle, an ex-Army lorry which we called 'Mephisto' and was painted pillar box red with an imposing devil painted on both doors. In Dunstable town we saw a forlorn group of girls standing by a bus stop, asked them whether they were nurses waiting to go to a dance and without further ado poured them into the back before returning triumphant to the site. An hour later an irate Matron from a hospital in Luton telephoned to ask when her nurses would be collected.

We had picked up the wrong ones, but after picking up the right ones we were very happy as it tipped the odds heavily in our favour.

The following Dunstable party firmly stated 'Evening Dress will be worn' so we went over dressed as Ancient Britons in hessian dyed in woad and wore straw hats. It was all very childish but good clean fun. *Esprit de corps* was a Surrey trait of which we were very proud. Flying up and down the Dunstable Downs was great, with the Whipsnade Zoo at its southern end where it was strongly inadvisable to land as the big cats roamed their large open-air pens looking upwards expectantly as you flew overhead. At the northern end is the bowl where, if you were below hill height, you had to execute a smart 180 degree turn. In front of the launch site the hill was sparsely covered by clumps of bushes which afforded discreet shelter for loving couples engaged 'in other forms of sport'. Indeed two very eminent glider pilots still claim to have warm recollections of the 'tunnels of love'. On one of our visits, a Surrey member attempted to hill soar when there was a distinct lack of wind blowing at the ridge. As he sank lower and lower and realised that he and the Tutor he was flying would soon be landing, he managed to shout a warning before flying into one of the bushes. The effect was electric, very similar to beaters putting up pheasants during a shoot except on this occasion he raised four birds of a different kind who with their partners were flushed out and ran off with their plumage in some disarray. Some time later something, possibly hungry rabbits, killed off the bushes and it was only years later before the love nests grew again.

When the London Club hosted the National Aerobatic Championship, one of our members gave a demonstration in his Slingsby Motor Tutor. This motorised version of the beloved Tutor could be fitted with either a 25 or 49 horsepower engine and to quote Fred Slingsby's words (see *British Gliders and Sailplanes* by Norman Ellison) "it was altogether a foolish and wasteful venture". As the pilot was flying up and down the hill, Cedric Vernon, then Chairman of the BGA Technical Committee, who was watching and realised that an accident was about to happen, told his two small children to look at something away from the hill just before the pilot and his aircraft met the hill in a most undignified manner. On being asked how he knew, Cedric replied "Well—I could see that the pilot was running out of height, speed and ideas all at the same time". The sequel to the prang is worth recording. Led by Rika, the pilot's wife, we ran up the hill fully expecting to find a mangled corpse. Rummaging through the wreckage we found the pilot happily hale and hearty seemingly only suffering from a severely dented ego. For good order and discipline however he was carted off to hospital for a check-up and when Rika was offered a seat in the car, she said that she would come on as soon as she had found her husband's teeth. A little later someone shouted "I've found them, here they are". Rika sped off to the hospital where himself was enjoying the attention of pretty nurses and when she said "Darling look, I got your teeth" he looked very surprised and answered "I don't know what you are talking about, I've got mine in my mouth". Whose teeth the other ones were we never did discover.

Back at home our Christmas parties gained a cultural dimension when the 'SODS'—the Surrey Operatic and Dramatic Society—was formed with two presiding men of genius and education, namely Messrs. Hugo Trotter and Pat Wood writing plays and songs. 'Wings for Prudence', a Victorian melodrama complete with a villain who was booed and the hero who was cheered by the audience, is a work worthy of the great Bard of Stratford himself and I recommend all gliding clubs to stage it. To that end and with scant regard to the authors' copyright, the complete script will be found at the end of this book. Similarly the Surrey song sheet is a mine of hysterical and historical interest and some other choice songs are also added at the end of this narrative. Pat Wood, the quite brilliant lyricist, wrote many of the Surrey Club songs but his best without doubt is the lament 'A Glider Pilot bold was he....'. Singing the songs on long winter evenings brought us members closer together and certainly helped to forge us into a strong and virile club.

We are the Surrey Gliders
Tune as The Church's one foundation

We are the Surrey Gliders,
What flaming good are we,
We are no good at winching,
We fumble with M.T.,
And when it comes to soaring,
We shout until we're pink,
Where are the flaming thermals,
There's only flaming sink

The gliding club's foundations,
Are Lorne and Mrs.D.,
They are the one salvation,
Of clueless types like me.
They put me in my glider,
They tow me on to track.
And when I'm in a claptrap,

They come and fetch me back

The gliding club's foundations,
Are Mrs.D. and Lorne,
They save us from frustration,
When we can't get airborne,
They take us to the clubhouse,
Whene'er the weather's fraught,
They buy us pints of cider,
And so they flaming ought

We are the London gliders,
We are the hillbound boys,
We are content to revel,
In orographic joys.
And if you should deride us,
We'll shout until we're blue,
That we've got dear Charles Ellis,
And Joan and Dudley too.

We are the trailer drivers,
We are "Mephisto's Own",
We are on hand to answer,
If you should telephone.
But if it's after nightfall,
Or if the outlook's bleak,
We'll only blow you raspberries,
And leave you "up the creek"

We are the Bar Committee,
We toil both night and day,
And everyone admits that,
We're socially O.K.
But should you break an ashtray,
Or should you drop your drink,
We'll take the little pieces,
And stuff them in the sink

Redhill attracted diverse gliding types like bees round a honey pot. One day a very proper gentleman arrived in his Rolls Royce, introduced himself—we called him Baron Divorce as his name sounded very much like that—and insisted that we teach his seventeen-year old daughter to glide. From the back of the Roller stepped an apparition who looked for all the world like Walt Disney's Sleeping Beauty with a delicate China Doll face, long flowing hair down to the tiny waist and dressed in the most immaculate white flying suit. The Baron insisted that only the Chief Flying Instructor could fly his darling daughter and invariably followed the launch in his Rolls Royce until they were safely off the ground. When she landed, he would speed over to the glider, order the child back into the car and stay there until it was her turn to have another launch. Lorne found the whole experience very unsatisfying as he was not able to brief and de-brief her but we were pretty sure that the baron did not really trust us. Sad to relate that after the girl had been airborne about twenty times, we never saw them again.

Another fascinating visitor was Group Captain Edward Mole who seemed to have an endless supply of the most beautiful young female companions. One cannot do justice to the man but to implore you to read his autobiography called *Happy Landings* with a sub-title; *The recollections of a light-hearted airman*. A founder member of the London Gliding Club, whose 'A' certificate, which he gained in 1930, is number No.6 on the British register, he had been sponsored by Barbara Cartland, then a young and beautiful woman on the threshold of her literary career. Surprisingly she claimed to have been the first person to suggest aero-towing as a way of launching gliders. Her aim was to win the 1931 Daily Mail prize for the first glider crossing of the English Channel. Unfortunately the Cirrus Moth tug could not climb towing the BAC VII higher than 6,000 feet and the attempt failed. In Edward's book there is a photograph of Dame Barbara standing by the glider which has her name in large letters painted on the cockpit sides. It is sad to reflect that now, sixty years later the Civil Aviation Authority, sometimes known as the Campaign Against Aviation, would regard that as aerial advertising and would probably order the name to be removed forthwith! Pity really, to-day the world is full of megalomaniacs who might be very eager to see their names on the sides of gliders and be prepared to pay big bucks for the privilege. The day after Mole's flight, Robert Kronfeld was towed to 12,000 feet over Boulogne in France and successfully crossed albeit east-west before repeating the feat but this time from England to France and thus collected the prize. It is worth recording that the first Channel crossing completed by a woman pilot was Joan Meakin's, one of Alan Cobham's Flying Circus stunt pilots, later Mrs. Ron Price, making her flight on 5 April 1934 when she was towed by a light aeroplane at 80 miles an hour.

The feat for which Edward Mole will always be remembered must surely be his world looping record. Although present day soaring pilots would find it hard to believe, feats such as duration records and the greatest number of continuous loops were then highly regarded. Even famous soaring pilots took part in these bouts. In 1936 Robert Kronfeld had set the record at 65 loops, an American upped this to 85 and in 1937 Wolf Hirth, the German designer of the Grunau Baby, had achieved 125 successive loops at the Stuttgart air show.

On 12 April 1938, Edward Mole, flying a Hungarian designed M.22 Turul, climbed to 15,400 feet towed by a Hawker Audax, the RAF light bomber of the day, and proceeded to loop 147 times taking twenty five minutes to complete them. His Commanding officer flew the 'chase' aircraft with official observers who had to verify each loop just in case the barograph did not record them properly. Not surprisingly on stepping out of the glider, Edward fell straight over backwards!

At Redhill we flew all the hours we could. Those of us who were members of the Royal Air Force Voluntary Reserve unit based there were in clover. We would fly gliders until 9 am, then go across the airfield to the VR office, sign the attendance book and fly Tiger Moths and later Chipmunks for an hour. Then back to gliding until 4pm when another hour's service flying completed your day's duty which qualified us for a day's pay, and then back to gliding for the remainder of the day. On non-cross-country days, it broke the tedium of intensive instructing and helped to pay for one's gliding. But, as life teaches you so often, it was too good to last.

With the RAFVR unit, the civilian flying club and the Surrey Gliding Club all increasing their activities very dramatically, the airfield owners decided to import a proper fully qualified Air Traffic Controller. All power flying was forced to use correct radio procedure and we could not launch a glider until a signal from an Aldis lamp flashing a green light for 'go' was given by the tower. Truth to tell, our new Trafficator was not one of our greatest fans, a sentiment which we heartily reciprocated. One day in 1950,

Ladi Marmol arrived overhead in his fully aerobatic Lunak L-107 sailplane and proceeded to give us a most spectacular display culminating in an inverted beat-up of the control tower just as our friend was flashing every red light he could find, but to no avail. Not only was Ladi one of the most celebrated display pilots, after two previous attempts in April 1949 he succeeded in establishing a new British Duration record by hill-soaring the Dunstable Downs for just over 33 hours. A week after Ladi's aerobatic arrival, an RAFVR Tiger Moth practising a blind take-off (where the pilot is under a canvas hood and a safety pilot or instructor sits in the rear seat) flew into our winch cable just after the glider had released. The Tiger corkscrewed down the wire and was severely bent though, the pilots were relatively undamaged.

A further incident which made us sit up and take notice of the shape of things to come was when Colonel Whitbread of beer fame ran into a brick wall whilst taxiing his private aeroplane on the airfield. The worthy ex-Army Major who had taken over as Secretary of the Flying Club was heard to say "Why didn't the fool take his foot off the accelerator?". The airfield was operated by British Air Transport Ltd. and this company was owned by the Douglas family. Before the war Ann Edmonds as she then was (later Douglas, then Welch) had flown with the London Gliding Club at Dunstable where all the cross country flights were started with hill soaring on the west facing hill and continued down-wind towards the Essex Coast. It was decided to find other hill sites in the South of England which faced other wind directions. As Ann wrote in an issue of the *Lasham Magazine* in the spring issue of 1973:

"There were the South Downs facing north, and the North Downs facing south; but the North Downs were a fine range of hills and between Dorking and Redhill in Surrey there were bits of hill that faced south west, and at Buckland there was a field large enough to winch from. On one SW wind day in the spring of 1938, we went there from Dunstable with five gliders and a bungey. We found a clear smooth patch of grass right on the edge of Colley Hill near Reigate and without further ado launched off. The locals were so astonished they forgot to object. We had a marvellous day but, for various very good reasons, Dunstable was not interested in starting another club there. I was! The hill gave good lift, in fact, the wind blew quite often from the south, and in any case the Buckland field was big enough to train from—if we could get it. But most encouraging of all was the enthusiasm of people who until now were too far from any gliding club. I knew we would get members all right, but the only person to begin with locally who knew anything about gliding was me.

With the supreme optimism of twenty-one years, an 'A' licence on Gipsy Moths, all of six months on Daglings, and ownership of a Grunau bought for £50, I got down to starting the Surrey Gliding Club. The owner of Redhill airfield, Graham Douglas, agreed to provide the capital necessary to buy the equipment: 1 hangar, 1 winch, 1 primary glider with spares, 1 Tutor with spares, 1 bungey, membership forms and log sheets etc. We bought everything for £300 and the first members erected the hangar. I found a couple of old bangers for cable retrieving and discovered someone willing to give us a substantial hut some 15 feet by 12 feet for a club house...". In 1930 there had been a very active and successful Surrey Gliding Club operating at Lockner Farm, Chilworth near Guildford but like many other small clubs it ceased operating a year later.

Both Ann and Graham excelled as flying instructors, with Ann, surely the ultimate dynamic and energetic gliding enthusiast carrying out the duties of the Chief Instructor of the gliding club, and Graham the CFI of the RAFVR unit at Redhill. They were both very attractive vibrant people and friendship soon led to marriage. Soon after the outbreak of war Graham was posted with the whole of the RAFVR No.15 Reserve Flying School to Carlisle and the now Mrs. Douglas joined the Air Transport Auxiliary as a ferry pilot delivering a wide range of military types of aircraft. When Graham, after a further period of instructing was posted to a fighter squadron and Ann was delivering Hurricanes and Spitfires, I wonder how many husband and wife teams were doing the same. One nice part of her story is that her eldest daughter flew in a Spitfire when she was only a very few weeks before her actual birth day.

By 1951, however, their marriage had, in flying parlance, run out of runway and with all the other goings on we decided that we had almost certainly out-stayed our welcome at Redhill. It was time to move on. Since 1949, we had realised that the day would come when due to collision hazards and considerable delays due to congestion we would have to find a new home. Ann and the Club Secretary, Dukinfield-Jones, were dispatched to talk to Airports Ltd. whose nearby airfield called Gatwick suited our purposes exactly. The talks went well but at the last moment the Ministry of Aviation stepped in and stopped us. It transpired that they had some long-term ambition to build a somewhat larger passenger airfield there on the site. We searched high and low for a suitable home for the next two years. Detling in Kent was too far, Smith's Lawn in Windsor Great Park too close to Heathrow, London's expanding airport. Blackbushe, just north of Farnborough in Hampshire, was dismissed because of the 'fraught' dilapidated buildings and we would not be in charge of the airfield. A number of other airfields were ruled out for various reasons.

The planning sub committee members reported that they were in favour of having our own site, that a field might do but preferably it should be an airfield, that airfields south of the Thames were out and that therefore an easily accessible site north east of London seemed the best bet. Just such an airfield was found, built during the war, good runways and grass, very dilapidated buildings but very near the end of the London Underground Terminus. It was called Chipping Ongar and is about 18 kilometres almost due south of what is now Stanstead International Airport!

On a large map we had plotted the homes of all our members to see whether we should go east or west. By a very few members, it seemed that going west would be more equitable which was most fortunate for the subsequent history of gliding in this country. Thankfully the gods smiled on us as we chose not Chipping Ongar airfield but decided on Lasham in Hampshire where the Army Gliding Club had the airfield all to themselves, having moved there from Odiham. Redhill had been a great home for us, our soaring fleet of one Weihe and four Olympias made us the best equipped club in the country and we took every advantage of the weather on each and every day. The members were a well balanced mix of wartime pilots, a large number of young people including students from the Imperial College of Science and Technology and many frustrated would-be pilots who, though mad keen to fly were not able to do so during the war for various reasons. This blend of experience and youth was highly beneficial to all, not only in matters of aviation but also the lively social activities in which we indulged.

By far the most important asset was the presence of our leader, mentor, teacher and friend, Lorne Welch. Without him we might just have been a fairly mediocre club. As most of our members had to earn a living and thus suffered serious withdrawal symptoms during the week, Hugo Trotter and I started a weekly lunch in a London Fleet Street hostelry called 'The Cock Tavern'. We soon attracted so many like-minded glider pilots that we moved, first to a Cypriot café close to Westminster Bridge where we drove the owner to despair by always insisting on 'corner baclava'. This Greek sweet is baked in large flat dishes and by demanding the corner pieces we ensured that we invariably got more than our fair share. When even that venue proved too small, we started the Kronfeld Club in a basement in Eccleston Square in Westminster. This proved an enormous success with lectures every week on very varied gliding and other aviation topics which were always a sell-out. As Hugo Trotter, Godfrey Harwood (the Surrey Club Treasurer) and his wife Rika, Peter Riddock the Secretary of the Surrey Club and Margaret and I all lived in the Square, we soon became known as the Eccleston Square Mob and were not the favourite people in Ann Welch's eyes as she was soon to make way for Hugo as the elected Chairman of the Surrey Club.

One day a number of talented members, including my wife, displayed some of their aviation paintings. Thus out of the Kronfeld Art Society grew the Guild of Aviation Artists, which continues to encourage, show and sell aviation art throughout the World.

In this and many other ways, ever egged on by Lorne Welch, the members gained great pleasure and satisfaction, not only in flying gliders, but also in helping to develop the sport in its widest sense for the good of all.

Good bye and Hallo
Words by Hugo Trotter
Tune as 'Jingle Bells'

Beaverettes, wireless sets,
Beans on buttered toast,
Locking wire, punctured tyre,
Halfway to the coast,

Jerry cans, frying pans,
Going to the Comps,
5 mile flights, boozy nights,
Little Hucklow romps

Auster tow, very slow,
Will we leave the ground,
Sewage farm, must keep calm,

Green ball gives a bound,
Thermal hats, yellow bats,
Bobbing up and down,
Wet week-end, round the bend,
Now we're hangar bound

Dunstable, unstable,
Sitting on the hill,
Wires are taut, things are fraught,
Blimey I feel ill,

Cable breaks, pilot shakes,
Does a dicey turn,
Landing ground, crunching sound,
Will he never learn.

Friston site, coastal flight,
Down to Beachy Head,
Seaford café, feel unsafe,
Two in single bed,

Cambridge town, cap and gown,
Auto-tows at Bourn,
Redhill 'drome, that's our home,
Filthy, tired and worn

V.R.kites, give us frights,
We are forced to go,
And we're found Hampshire bound,
Beaverettes in tow,

Golden Pot, just the spot,
Lasham is quite near,
Army types, smoking pipes,
Watney's Alton beer

Chapter 10

The Lasham airfield history

The Lasham lands have a most fascinating history which deserves to be fully recorded by someone better qualified than this author. The village and the adjacent airfield are perched on a hill six hundred feet above sea level in north east Hampshire, an area of England rich in historical sites and ruins dating back to the Norman Conquest in 1066. Local history goes back even further as we discovered when a *Times* newspaper photographer took a picture of Tony Deane-Drummond practising over Lasham before the start of the 1957 National Championships. When the superb air to air shot of the glider was published, under one wing in the field below was clear evidence of a round barrow of pre-Roman times which until then nobody had known was there. People have lived in the area since the early Bronze age. The Lasham area formed part of Edward the Confessor's Crown lands and is named in the Doomsday Book. By 1086, after the Norman Conquest twenty years earlier, it was assessed at two and a half hides. From then on there were many changes of tenant who were, of course, the Lords of the Manor. In 1314 Walter de Aberval was granted 'a messuage' and land in Lessham to hold for his life, promising in addition to "provide the King with two robes worth forty shillings every year as long as he lived". That must have been a veritable fortune in those days and one wonders what other service he was obliged to offer his Royal landlord. What would Walter de Aberval have said had he known that nearly seven hundred years later his successors to the Lasham Lands, the members of the Lasham Gliding Society, were paying as rent one peppercorn a year (but only if called for), to the Crown?. It is only fair to mention that during the interval of the thirty Kings and Queens who have sat on the throne since 1314, the lands still designated as 'Crown property' actually belong to 'The State' and LGS in 1989 bought a lease from 'The State' of part of the lands for a 'consideration' amounting to £180,000. Perhaps some clever clogs could tell us which amount is the greater in real purchasing power; the forty shillings in 1314 or the nearly £200,000 which includes the lawyers and other costs we paid in 1991 although the lease was backdated to 1989?

Earlier, in 1297, the 3rd Earl of Ulster had taken possession and when

Edward Plantagenet, the tenth Earl of Ulster and 4th Duke of York ascended the throne in 1461 as Edward IV, the Lasham lands were combined with the Royal Castle of Odiham. In 1775 the Jervoise (pronounced Jarvis) family who, through marriage had held the adjoining Manor of Herriard since the early part of the 13th Century, bought the Lasham Manor and the enlarged estate has been in their possession ever since. When we arrived at Lasham, the then Squire, Major Francis Henry Tristram Jervoise was a splendid character who not only took great pride in his estate but was a most enlightened employer and landowner. The lot of his tenants and the quality of his fields were greatly improved by the water piped by the Herriard and Lasham Water Company which he created. He continued the family tradition of planting a great number of trees and was very upset when the contractors building the airfield in 1942 cut down a large number of the beech trees. These lined the Avenue which runs for a mile along the northern side of the airfield and had been planted by George Jervoise in 1809. Our Squire had a flock of Black Welsh mountain sheep and all his suits were made of homespun cloth using their wool. When coming back to Lasham by air or by road, the sight of those black sheep in the field of Herriard Park always gave me a warm glow and the certain knowledge that home was only half a mile away.

The pronunciation and indeed spelling of Lasham has changed over the years. It was Esseham in the 11th Century, Lessham in the 12th, Lesseham, Lasseham, Lassham and Lassam up to the 16th. Soon after starting flying at Lasham, we went to call on the Squire in order to explain who we were, what we were about and promising to behave. The first time I said 'Lasham' in what is now accepted as the normal pronunciation, the Squire exploded and said " Boy, it is LASSAM, it has always been LASSAM and don't you ever forget it!". When some time later Raymond Baxter, Brian Johnston and I did the first of many live BBC outside broadcasts from Lasham we were most careful to get the pronunciation right but unfortunately the BBC announcer introducing the programme undid our good work. The Squire was on the 'phone like a flash and ordered me to tell 'those Broadcasting fellahs' to correct their mistake. Some of the locals still use the correct 'Lassam' to this day, over the years some glider pilots have been known to pronounce it 'Splasham', but in the main, the rest of the world calls it 'Lasham'.

Most of the land is heavy clay with a chalk subsoil and was farmed growing crops chiefly wheat, oats and turnips. Before the First World War various Army cavalry units used it for training manoeuvres and gallops. To this day there is a group of cottages just north of the airfield in Southrope still known as 'The Barracks'. The senior recorded ghost who is said to roam the airfield is a cavalryman astride a horse and wearing a long coat! The other one is said to be that of a Polish Mosquito pilot in full flying gear who was killed close to the airfield. After fifty-plus years at Lasham I have never seen either ghost but would love to be the third one when my time comes. What fun I could have....!

The airfield was built in late 1942 and early 1943 and the first aircraft landed there in March 1943. On 2 January 1943 the German Luftwaffe sent a Dornier bomber to strafe, bomb and harass the builders. Our High Command quickly got the message and sent an advance party from No. 4165 Anti-Aircraft Flight which duly arrived on the 10th of January. There are many stories told about the construction period. The place must have resembled the Tower of Babel as Canadian, Irish and English and Italian and other prisoners of war were engaged in the building work. A murder, mayhem, black market activities—especially in the 'Golden Pot'—and other events will hopefully be recorded one day and will make fascinating reading.

On commissioning in March 1943 as a Fighter Command airfield, the first operational unit was No.175 Squadron, then equipped with Hawker Hurricane IIBs. Then various Spitfire and Typhoon squadrons were there until in August of that year when Lasham was transferred to the 2nd Tactical Air Force. It become the home of 2 Group's No.138 Wing. This consisted of the Dutch No. 320, the Polish No. 305 and RAF No. 613 Squadrons, later to be joined by No.107, all equipped with Mosquitoes. A wide variety of targets were on the receiving end of the 138 Wing punch. The concrete launching ramps of the pilotless V.1 'doodlebug' which were springing up all over the place behind the French coast were favourite targets and the code name given to these raids showed that even in war some people still have a sense of humour. They were called 'The Noball sites'. But the most dramatic and famous operation took place on 11 April 1944 when Wing Commander Bob Bateson led six Mosquitoes of 613 Squadron on a raid designed to destroy the Kuntzall Art Gallery in the centre of The Hague in Holland. The building, which housed the Dutch Central Population Registry, where the Gestapo kept records of Dutch families for reprisal purposes, had five floors and was ninety five feet high. Bateson was ordered to destroy the building but not to damage the houses on either side and this he and his crews accomplished to the letter.

In the autumn of 1944, No. 138 Wing moved from Lasham, leaving the airfield temporarily unoccupied, to Hartfordbridge (now called Blackbushe) which No. 137 Wing (in which I was a very minor player) had vacated on our move to Vitry-en-Artois in France. Of the few days I spent at Lasham on detachment in late August 1944, all that really comes to mind were the visits to the dingy 'beer and cider only' public house called 'The Royal Oak' in Lasham village. The 'Oak' is still going strong, producing very nourishing food, a vast variety of intoxicating fluid and has an extremely friendly atmosphere. All in all a great village pub, well worth a visit.

At the end of 1944, the airfield reverted to Fighter Command who used it as the Disbandment Centre before closing on 26 October 1948. David Ince in his very readable book, *Combat and Competition,* in which he details his experiences as a wartime Fighter Pilot, then a civilian test pilot through to his gliding days, wrote:

"On 7 September 1945 I led my (No.193) Squadron back to England to Lasham where we carried out a final stream landing. In the dispersals they were doing dreadful things to an earlier batch of Typhoons. Wings and fuselages, stripped to bare shells, were being lined up in closely packed rows and bulldozed together, for all the world like a giant scrap baling press. Tomorrow, or the day after, our aircraft would be under the hammer".

During March 1945, General Aircraft Ltd took over two of the four large T.2. hangars, the dimensions of which are 240 feet by 120 feet, and some of the other buildings to carry out contracts for the maintenance and conversion of Mosquitoes and other types of aircraft. Later they were to carry out flight trials of their experimental tailless gliders. In the winter of 1948 Chipperfield Circus occupied the western hangar and during a particularly cold spell one of their elephants died. It appears that they dug a very large hole and buried the poor beastie there. Surely Lasham must be the only airfield in the world which can boast an elephant grave and one wonders what future archaeologists will think when they excavate our site and find bombs, bullets and an elephant skeleton! Rumours are still rife about the various 'goodies' buried in the dell behind the main control tower including, it is alleged, two brand new Merlin engines.

The Army Gliding Club based at the RAF Odiham airfield was able to organise a few courses at Lasham in 1948 and 1949 and in June 1950, under the guidance and Chairmanship of Tony Deane-Drummond, then an Instructor at the Royal Military Academy Sandhurst, moved its operation to

Lasham permanently. Of the four T.2. hangars at Lasham, the northern one (which has since been demolished) was still in use by General Aircraft Ltd. The one currently used as the gliding hangar was in such a poor state of repair that it was not even considered; the southern one was deemed to be too remote, but the one recently vacated by the Circus was not only in excellent repair but also still had an ample supply of clean hay in one corner which came in very useful when derigging gliders without trailers.

In August 1951 Surrey and Imperial College members moved all our goods and chattels, which loosely meant anything that was not screwed down, and we established ourselves at Lasham.

Alan Purnell in a Skylark flying over Lasham in 1960

Chapter 11

Robert Kronfeld

Very many famous glider pilots have flown from Lasham and many more will surely do so in the future, but no one will be able to outclass one of the greatest of them all. It is a remarkable quirk of fate that Lasham, which has developed as the largest gliding centre in the world, should be the very place from which Robert Kronfeld took off for the last flight of his life. The fatal crash occurred on February 12, 1948 at Lower Froyle, just three miles east of the Airfield. Born in Vienna on May 5, 1904, his early passions were his violin, skiing and mountain climbing. He also achieved great fame in his kayak before being bitten by the gliding bug in 1927. By the following year he was an instructor at the Wasserkuppe, which was by then the Mecca for all glider pilots. He was the first to realise that up-currents below cumulus clouds could be used to achieve cross-country flights and quickly established new world distance records. He is credited with the development of the variometer which some of his competitors initially regarded as a form of cheating. As soon as the instruments were readily available to others, the jealousy ceased. He was also the first pilot to climb in a thunderstorm when in 1929 he doubled the world height record.

When, in February 1931, the *Federation Aeronautique Internationale* instituted the Silver 'C' badge, Kronfeld, Hirth and Groenhoff were the first three recipients. The accounts of his pioneering flights make fascinating reading for the modern pilot who tends to take high performance and sophisticated instrumentation for granted. His book, *Kronfeld on Gliding and Soaring*, is an absolute masterpiece but regretfully copies are extremely hard to find.

The Austria, designed and built for him in 1932 specifically for very efficient hill soaring with a span of thirty metres, broke up in cloud when violent up-currents caused the wing tips to break off, forcing him to escape by parachute. Later, in his beloved Wien, a mere twenty metre span glider, he carried out a great number of spectacular flights.

He came to England in 1933 as a refugee from Nazi persecution and over the next few years gave gliding demonstrations in the USA and all over Europe. In May 1933 he used a most dramatic thermal by soaring over Mount Vesuvius during an eruption and had by that year completed over 10,000km in aero-towed flights on his way to various assignments. He was the first pilot to soar across the top of the Matterhorn, a feat repeated by his son Bill in 1963. In June 1938 he was appointed manager and Chief Instructor of the new Oxford University & City Gliding Club and at the outbreak of the war a year later joined the Royal Air Force. He was soon posted to a very strange unit mis-named 'The Central Landing School' at Ringway near Manchester, now Manchester International Airport, the pride of the North! The story of the unit has been recorded by Laurence Wright, he of the Pyramid spoof, in his book *The Wooden Sword.* As this chapter is meant as a tribute to Robert Kronfeld, I asked Mike Maufe who worked closely with him and all the other glider pilots who had also been brought to Ringway to let us share some of his memories. Not only did Mike come up trumps but furthermore added his 'Memories of Ringway 1940-1942'. He wrote: "Enclosed is a copy of my 'Memories' which I found. It will give some idea of the sort of work which we were involved in during the war but not too much about Robert himself. Although we shared an office, he was very reserved and I never got to know him intimately. After dinner in the Officers Mess, he would nearly always go straight back to his room. He was dedicated to his work, both to his test flying and the technical calculations and reports which he produced. For instance, I have no doubt that his report on the very primitive Tow Cable Angle Indicator (affectionately known as 'The Angle of Dangle') which we built in our workshop will have influenced the final design produced by RAE Farnborough. With his long and meritorious prewar gliding experience and high technical qualifications, Robert was the ideal choice for Chief Test Pilot in the Airborne Forces Experimental Establishment and his Air Force Cross was well deserved. I was privileged to have flown with him. He was 'reserve' best man for our wedding in case my young brother couldn't get leave for it!"

A few short extracts from 'Memories of Ringway 1940-1942' by Mike Maufe (Silver 'C' No.40 and a leading light of the Vintage Glider Club) state: "When I arrived at Ringway in November 1940 I found that the unit included over a dozen pre-war glider pilots, several of whom I knew. Apparently, we were the 'founder members' of a future Airborne Force ordered to be formed by Winston Churchill when he heard that the German Army had captured a vital fort in Belgium using glider borne troops. The Central Landing School consisted of a Parachute Training School and a Tactical Development Unit commanded by Wing Commander 'Mungo' Buxton, the well known glider designer and pilot, and to which unit I was posted. From this was later on formed the Glider Training School which moved down to RAF Thame near Aylesbury early in 1941 where the Army glider pilots were trained. The Chief Test Pilot was Robert Kronfeld with whom I was to work very closely, and frequently fly with. Other members of the unit, all glider pilots were: Norman Sharpe, the Chairman of the Yorkshire Gliding Club; Tim Hervey, former Manager and then Chief Instructor of the London Club; Lawrence Wright the architect; Robin Fender; Pat Pringle; 'Pop' Furlong; 'Wilkie' Wilkinson and a number of others. The only aircraft we had to begin with were all requisitioned privately owned or club gliders: Philip Wills's Minimoa, the 'Rhonbussard' belonging to the Pasold brothers, Eustace Thomas's 'Condor', Roy Scott's 'Viking' and three Kirby Kites. A Viking two-seater was also at Ringway for a short time until it shed its wings during an unauthorised display of aerobatics by Wilkinson. Another twelve Kirby Kites were allocated to the Glider Training School. It can easily be imagined that the atmosphere at Ringway was more like that of a civilian gliding club than a normal service unit, which tended to cause some friction with the Regular Service Officers. For instance, when the pilots, who knew quite a lot about gliders, tried to pass them out as airworthy themselves, they were told that this should only be done by qualified technical personnel who at that time knew nothing about gliders! Furthermore trying to get glider pilots to perform routine drill movements smartly proved to be impossible and eventually they were excused parades".

At the first meeting of the British Gliding Association held after the war, Robert Kronfeld represented the Oxford Club and thus helped Dudley Hiscox the Chairman to restart the Association's sterling work for the movement which has continued ever since. On leaving the Air Force he joined General Aircraft Ltd. as the Chief Test Pilot to research the flight characteristics of tailless gliders. Four types, designated GA 56 Mark 1 to Mark 4 were built. Captain Eric 'Winkle' Brown, the former Chief Naval Test Pilot and Commanding Officer of the renowned Aerodynamics Flight at the Royal Aircraft Establishment, Farnborough, and who is listed in the Guinness Book of Records as having flown more types of aircraft than any other pilot in the world, describes flying them in his book, *Wings of the Weird & Wonderful,* as "..the worst aircraft I have ever flown". On 12 February 1948, Kronfeld and his Observer, Barry MacGowan, took off from Lasham and were towed to 17,000 feet behind a Halifax four engined bomber. It is interesting to note that a Spitfire Mark IX was used as the tug aircraft when Winkle Brown was testing the GA 56 at Farnborough. While carrying out highly dangerous stall manoeuvres, the aircraft failed to respond to any recovery action. Barry MacGowan sitting in the rear seat behind Kronfeld writes:

"Things happened very rapidly, and when I resumed my technical interest, I saw that we were going straight down at 200 knots! At this stage Robert realised that the machine was out of control and decided to abandon ship. In reconstruction, it appeared that the rapid dive after the stall, with the elevator trimmer at fully forward, resulted in the build up of large forward stick forces which were overpowering. Calculations suggested that Robert was pulling back with up to 80 pounds, yet the aircraft was still accelerating. The first action to escape was to reach up to jettison the canopy. In so doing he would have lost about 30 pounds pull back on the stick. Again, later calculations suggested that would have resulted in an immediate 5G negative. Certainly, the next thing I remembered was my portable oxygen bottle hurtling past my left side, and crashing into the canopy. At that stage we both 'redded-out' in this negative G. Presumably as Robert became unconscious, and released all his grip, more negative G followed.

I am perpetually grateful to G.A.L's designers that in spite of probably being above VNE, the aircraft remained in one piece and absorbed such a punishment. At some later stage, I briefly recovered consciousness. The aircraft was upside down, perfectly stable, and certainly not in a spin. I realised that Robert was also still in the aircraft, not answering, but I could not get to him in the tandem cockpit arrangement, separated as we were by a substantial structure. I didn't seem to make any conscious attempt to move, and 'redded out' again. Then some time later, quite automatically, and literally in an unseeing red haze, I found myself jettisoning the canopy, releasing the seat harness, falling straight out of the upside down TS507 and pulling the rip cord. The opening jerk of the 'chute cleared my eyes, so that I was able to see to land. The great tragedy of the affair was that Robert must never have recovered consciousness at all. This was later related just to his age. The one consolation to us all is that he certainly was never aware of the descent or crash and therefore did not suffer any fear or pain."

The glider crashed at 11.45 into a field. Strangely, Robert Kronfeld died just a few days after that other great pioneer of flying, Orville Wright. Wolf Hirth wrote a full and very sensitive obituary, which concluded:

"After twenty fruitful years of devotion to the cause of human flight this great and good man had been granted an airman's sudden splendid death. His name like his deeds will never be forgotten. Robert Kronfeld lives on in every soaring flight".

He would have been delighted to know that Robert's son Bill and his grandson, Simon, are both very active Lasham based Gold 'C' pilots—thus the wonderful family tradition continues in safe hands. Robert Kronfeld's legacy to us glider pilots is incalculable.

Soaring techniques, instructing, aero-towing, powered gliders, instrumentation to name but a few were some aspects of our sport which he invented and developed—no man has ever done more.

The permanent Kronfeld memorial in the Lasham clubhouse. There is a small brass plaque which reads "Robert Kronfeld 1904-1948. The International Gliding pioneer and World Record holder whose expertise led to the development of soaring flight and the modern gliding movement. He lost his life testing a military glider at Lasham

Chapter 12

Lasham

At Redhill we were spoilt with running water, flushing lavatories, a squash court, a comfortable wooden clubhouse and the three very friendly bars on the airfield which often provided splendid entertainment and highly amusing characters. None of us will forget some of the Surrey Flying Club members such as Ted the wealthy butcher, whose girlfriend was the extremely well built Ada (our parachute packer), and the Public Relations gent, who insisted on handing over endless five-pound notes in their bar so that all present could quench their thirst until they were totally legless. His girl friend was a model in the 'knickers and bras' world much in demand by us and Dudley Hiscox's company called 'Ambrose Wilson' which specialised in very artistic mail order catalogues of lingerie items. Thus the superb flying facilities were amply augmented by the flying equivalent of 'apres ski'.

Lasham, however, was something else. We knew that we would have to start from scratch and so 'liberated' (a wartime euphemism for pinching though not really considered as stealing) anything considered of possible use at our new home. One raiding party at Redhill put an end to this when I was despatched to retrieve a wooden door which was lying on the floor of a long abandoned Nissen hut on the far side of the airfield. Not wishing to be too obvious, I tied a long piece of old winch cable to the door, the other end to a Beaverette and proceeded to drive back to our hangar. Well pleased with this ploy, which I felt certain would not be noticed, life came to an abrupt and sticky end when a large motor car being driven by old man Douglas, Graham's father, came alongside. He demanded to know what the hell was going on. Apparently, he had come on to the airfield by an old road which was hardly ever used to be confronted by the cable that should not have been there moving across the ground. Somewhat puzzled he sat there until suddenly the door appeared. To say that he was not best pleased would be a major understatement.

Wood for doors and other building works was essential and luckily a friend who had just closed a very old fashioned tobacco shop in Pall Mall agreed to give us all the wood panelling and anything else we wanted. We hurried up to town with a glider trailer and in next to no time the shop was bare and the trailer was very very full. In those days our police force did not like or understand glider trailers. Indeed, in their little black book it stated that they were considered too long to be towed on public roads behind private vehicles. Whenever we were stopped by a keen young constable we would explain that a glider was an indivisible load, refer the officer to page 78 of his police book and proceed merrily on our way. That is fine if you do not happen to be driving in a Royal Park, and Hyde Park in London is so designated. "Stop" said your man in blue "Don't you know you can't tow commercial trailers behind private cars and what's more no commercial vehicles are allowed to use the roads in Royal Parks". Quick as a flash someone said "But Officer, it is an indivisible load, to wit a glider". "Let's see it" said the law. "Sorry, we can't show it to you, we have lost the key and have to go back to Hampshire to get the glider out". Thankfully he believed us but we learnt yet another valuable lesson. When moving things other than gliders in a trailer, don't drive through Hyde Park!

The Cambridge Club did not learn from our experience. Professor John Pringle was offered a dead whale which had died on an Essex beach. Being Chairman of the Cambridge Club he asked his CFI Ken Machin to collect it for him. Off went Ken with another club member and in no time the whale was safely stowed inside their glider trailer. On the way home while still in the County of Essex, they were stopped by the law. "Don't you know that towing a long trailer behind a private vehicle is illegal" said the man in blue. Quick as a flash, Ken replied "If you look in your little black book, you will see that glider trailers are exempt, they are covered under the section dealing with indivisible loads". "Oh, it"s a glider in there, lets see it". "Well actually, officer, not this time, it's a dead whale". The policeman was somewhat taken aback, threatened to charge them for trying to make a fool of him, contravening a Ministry of Food byelaw concerned with the transport of dead animals and lastly what he thought was his trump card, the use of a glider trailer towed by a private vehicle. He then took his little black book out of his pocket but unfortunately it did not contain the relevant section. When he was shown and smelled the dead whale, he gave up and let them off with a severe wigging. As they drove into Cambridgeshire, they were stopped again by another policeman. "Don't worry, officer" Ken said, "you need't look in your little black book, the section on indivisible loads is not in there". "That's all right" said the arm of the law, "I've got the big black book with me, let's see if we can find it there!". Happily it is in the big book.

At Lasham we had taken over the secondary tower as our clubhouse and everyone set to with a vengeance. First we built a splendid bar on the first floor and Lionel Alexander, then not yet the Prosecuting Barrister of the Crime Department of the Inland Revenue, pleaded our case in front of the Licensing Magistrates. "All they have as a bar are two beer crates and a plank of wood" he told them and they believed him! As we had no running water it was decided to purloin a 400 gallon water tank and site it over the stairs on two concrete beams which Dick Watson made specially. Three times we carried the damn thing up, three times Lorne Welch vetoed the idea as he reckoned the building was not strong enough. So we waited until he went home, took it back up again and cemented the beams into position.

Dick Watson at that time worked for the Concrete Development Company so he knew a thing or two. He is a great guy who was always pressed into service as the head cook on our gliding expeditions. The story of how he met his delightful wife is worth recording. One day while going to work by London Underground he saw a filly who immediately made him sit up and take notice. He caught the same train the next day and there she was again. Being very shy he decided to sit opposite her and let her know all about himself. The first day he read the *Concrete Engineer*, the next the Imperial College students magazine, then *Sailplane and Gliding* and soon Jean, the object of his affection, caught on and started with *The Nursing Gazette*, *The Physiotherapist Journal* and other revealing papers. As he carried an attaché case which bore his initials 'R.V.W.' she decided that he must be called 'RipVan Winkle'. Some weeks later they happened to literally bump into each other and actually spoke. The rest as they say is history. One day Dick mentioned that a friend of his mother's had an upright piano which was surplus to requirements and wondered whether we would like it for Lasham. No sooner offered and we were off with an open tipper truck which Dick borrowed from work to collect the piano from a very posh house in Chelsea. After thanking our benefactor and promising to take good care of her pride and joy, though in truth rather dilapidated, we loaded up and off we went. The temptation was too much for us and we decided to take turns playing the piano whilst being driven round Piccadilly Circus. We managed three laps before we were forcibly moved on and warned never to do that again. It was by then rather late in the day and Dick offered to park the truck outside his family home in St.John's Wood. As his stepfather was the most senior civil servant in the Air Ministry he thought that none of the neighbours would object.

Next morning a young policeman knocked on the door and asked Lady Campbell whether she knew anything about one tipper truck plus piano parked in her very select area of London. "Must be my son's, no problem, don't worry" was her reply. When we got it down to Lasham, sad to relate, it only survived one party before some drunks threw it down the stairs.

Throwing out of tune pianos down concrete stairs makes a lovely noise and will enliven any party. Thereafter we collected old pianos wherever we could and they became an essential part of our entertainment.

The lack of running water was a serious problem as emptying Elsan buckets was not a popular pastime and our girls, who performed miracles in our makeshift kitchen, were getting decidedly stroppy. A chance visit to a machinery exhibition produced the solution. I spotted a large gleaming piece of machinery which for all I knew could be making railway engines or something equally bizarre until at the back of the monster it became all too clear what the final product was. Out of a hole came yard after yard of black plastic piping which was being fed onto a huge roller . "Are you interested in our latest machine?" asked a salesman. Before I could answer, the sales manager spotted me; in those days I was wearing regulation City gear complete with bowler hat and rolled umbrella and he obviously thought that anyone dressed in that garb was either very important or someone from Head Office, and came rushing over. "No Sir, your machine is quite splendid, but to be honest I am interested in what it is making" and before he had a chance of going off, I launched into "We are a poor gliding club, helping the young especially University students to sample flying, our place in the world, the need to encourage air mindedness—remember the Battle of Britain etc etc" and finishing up with "What are you going to do with all that black piping you are making when the exhibition is over?". Happily a deal was struck and we finished up with two miles of lovely two inch diameter black plastic piping which we had laid from a mains at Avenue Farm to the clubhouse at a total cost of less than £500. It is still in use to this day.

Now we were in business and not only altered our lavatory called 'Palazzo Elsano' into a fully flushing luxury privy but also set about the soak-away problem. A huge hole was called for and Colonel John Lathbury persuaded some of the Royal Military Academy Sandhurst cadets to help dig it. It was to be a mammoth hole, 15 feet by 10 feet and 10 feet deep and we warned the young gentlemen that John was a very strict disciplinarian who knew the Commandant of their Academy very well. In fact John was a pussy cat but we wanted the hole dug with no slacking. By the time the hole was seven feet deep, all the young lads had dropped from exhaustion except one who was determined not be beaten. He was Simon Marriott and he has proved his worth to Queen, the Country and the Gliding movement ever since. It is said that he is the only person who can keep Ralph Jones in order—a rare feat indeed. It was Simon who crewed for that real tiger, Tony Deane-Drummond, in the National Championships the following year . On being asked what it was like said "It was rather like being a juryman in a murder trial, once you have done it, you should be exempt for life!".

In order to keep our flying fees to a minimum, and to avoid spending money unnecessarily, all the members were persuaded to undertake even the most menial and boring jobs. One such which was not very popular was the 'Beaverette run-in'. After every overhaul or engine change, the Beaverettes which we used for cable towing had to be driven very carefully at no more than thirty miles an hour for five hundred miles until the engine had been adequately 'run-in'. It required sixteen members each taking a one hour stint, driving round the airfield to complete the task.

Mike Neale, who was our mechanical transport genius, decided that it would be more fun to drive the Beaver down to Cornwall and back. Off he went with another Imperial College member as co-driver. When they reached Exeter early in the morning, they found themselves stopped right behind a policeman on point duty at a cross-road.

Cut down armoured cars are not often seen in the City of Exeter and our man in blue was eager to add to his fund of knowledge. As he approached he stopped, sniffed the air and then saw a sight which was not in the policeman's training syllabus. Mike was busily cooking bacon and eggs on a primus stove. "What the bloody hell, what do you think you are doing?"Cooking breakfast" said Mike "would you like some?". Having crewed in various World Championships, Mike decided that in order to improve VHF radio communication, he would design and build a telescopic aerial. At this point it is necessary to explain that he is a very famous tribologist in great demand all over the world. In case you do not know the definition of tribology, it is the science and technology of surfaces in relatively moving contact.

So Mike built his device. Four sections sliding on nylon guide strips, each ten feet high made of best quality strong timber. The seals were made using domestic draught excluder and the whole structure weighed about 3 cwt.The erection method was to attach a pipe to the bottom of the aerial and the other end to the exhaust pipe of Mike's Jaguar. The initial tests were carried out in secret but everyone was eager to be present for the final test. "Start the engine, increase the revs." Nothing happened. "More revs—still more". Suddenly the first smallest section appeared, shuddered and disappeared again. Mike shouted at the poor unfortunate in the Jaguar, "Give it everything—now!". The top section rose majestically and just as the next section appeared, there was an enormous bang and the car's core plugs shot out.

Mike's next invention was a mechanical hair washing-machine which didn't work either.

An extract from Doc. Slater's 'Gliding Notes' published in *The Aeroplane* issue of 2 January 1953 reports: "Lasham's Christmas party was in the established tradition of the Surrey and Imperial Clubs, with that of the Army Gliding Club thrown in. The blackboard announced a full programme from 'Bar Opens' at 17.00 hours Saturday to 'Hot Dogs and Coffee' at 04.00 hours on Sunday. Highlights were the brewing of punch at 19.00, fancy dress contest at 19.15, and pantomime at 20.30. The panto entitled 'Ikkle Rude Gliding Bed' started with an air-minded young lady cycling towards the London Gliding Club. But the signpost, pointing to Dunstable one way and Lasham the other, had been wickedly reversed by two witches from the Surrey Club, and our fair gliding aspirant soon found herself in the Lasham kitchen. The fancy dress theme was 'What would you do if you couldn't glide?'. There were at least two suicides,one of whom, a determined character, had a rope round his neck, a pistol to his head, a dagger in his breast and a brick tied round his middle. Tony Goodhart arrived as a skeleton with the notice saying 'No Gliding, No Living'. The winners of the most appropriate costume competition were Beryl and Geoffery Stephenson, the first man to soar across the English channel, who came over from Dunstable. They announced that they came as 'husband and wife', a subtle message which was not lost on other gliding spouses present!"

The speed of increase in both members and flying was beginning to be more than we could handle without permanent staff. Even our darling wives who cooked nourishing lunches and dinners for the hungry mob under the most appallingly primitive conditions gave us their ultimatum—you men must help us or find a local cook or else... They only played that card once for immediately the Chairman, Hugo Trotter, announced that on the following Saturday roles would be reversed. Supper would be cooked by the men and the girls could wash up instead. He and Cliff Dowdall then set to work amid great secrecy and everyone wondered what feast would be set before us when we finished flying. As everyone rushed back to the clubhouse, the smell of the food was wonderful and we knew that it would be a meal to remember. It was! The potatoes were dyed red, the meat blue, the carrots green and the cabbage a dreadful mouse colour. Thereafter it was decreed that only women would be allowed to cook at Lasham—that was until 'Dandruff George' came along. We had divided the Committee responsibilities into two areas, each under its own Chairman: 'inside peritrack' and 'outside peritrack'. Finding keen, well qualified members to serve on the 'outside' Committee known as 'Lasham Living' was no problem but we realised that a very special person was required to take over the role of Resident Flying Instructor and help the 'inside' boys do their job more effectively.

Derek Piggott about to fly the replica Cayley

Chapter 13

Derek Piggott—our hero!

By 1954, the Army Club who had been flying at Lasham since 1950, agreed to combine their flying operations with us. By this time the Surrey and the Imperial College of Science and Technology Clubs had been joined by the Polish Air Force Association Gliding Club, whose members were a splendid public-spirited, hard working bunch of rugged individualists, and the Leighton Park Boys School of Reading gliding section who had built themselves a Slingsby T.21 two-seater under the supervision of John Simpson. To make this amalgamation of fiercely independent clubs and people work, we realised that we would need a paragon as the resident Flying Instructor.

We found just the man in Alan Derek Piggott who at that time was still serving in the Royal Air Force acting as the Chief Instructor at the Detling Gliding School. When he finally retired from Lasham in 1989, an article written by me for the Lasham magazine said:

"OUR HERO! Back in the dark ages when we still enjoyed superb soaring summers and most of you, dear Readers, were not even born, I was lucky enough to do something which has since benefited countless thousands of my fellow human beings throughout the world." I met, admired, and finally persuaded Alan Derek Piggott to leave the Royal Air Force and join us.

My letter to him of 20 September 1953 said: "My dear Alan, With reference to our conversation at Farnborough, I have told our Committee that you might be interested in the position of Resident Flying Instructor of the Surrey Gliding Club. With this in mind, I am authorised by our Committee to ask you whether you will consider the following offer: That you come to us at a salary of not less than £700 per year, that all your flying will be free but that you will have to pay for your own retrieving and aero-tows. Time off, holidays etc, will be by arrangement. The club at the moment operates one Weihe, four Olympias, two two-seaters and one Tutor. We have just tendered for two Tiger Moths. We are further looking for a full-time aircraft-cum-MT ground engineer. The Club is also looking for a lady to operate the catering arrangements who will be paid two shillings an hour.".

I blush on re-reading this letter for many reasons, some more obvious than others! When you think that Derek's final salary from us was probably not much more in real terms than the £700 we offered him thirty five years earlier, it makes you realise how financially shabbily the gliding movement rewards the very people who make it possible for us to enjoy our sport. No apologies for mentioning one of my hobby horses which, together with security of tenure, fund raising to be able to pay for our freehold when it comes, and democratic justice have been major factors in my life. But to go on about Derek, who changed his name when he joined us, but that's another story. No one can do adequate justice to the man. The stories he tells about his stunt flying in films such as 'Those Magnificent Men in their Flying Machines', 'Blue Max', 'Chitty Chitty Bang Bang', 'Darling Lili' and numerous others will make the hairs on the back of your neck stand bolt upright! The only real way is for him to write the unexpurgated version of his life as a follow up to his autobiography 'Delta Papa'. When Derek joined us at the beginning of 1954 he brought Warren Storey, a superb glider mender with him; we found a cook and Lasham has never looked back. Without ADP we could not have built Lasham into what it is to-day. He was the engine and the fuel that made us go. His boundless energy, enthusiasm and flying perfection inspired us all to work for the common cause, help new and young members to learn and love our sport and always fly better, safer, higher and further. My friend Godfrey Smith in his *Sunday Times* column quoted Emerson the other day. Something like "Heroes are in danger of becoming bores to succeeding generations". That will never be true of Derek. For years to come pilots the world over will be able to boast that their instructor or their instructor's instructor was the great Derek Piggott. During his life Derek has been honoured by almost everyone: the Queen, the FAI, the Royal Aero Club, the BGA and countless other worthy bodies. He has won model aircraft awards, gliding awards, flying awards, filming awards and more besides, any one of which would have satisfied and delighted more ordinary mortals. His collection of diverse gongs is well worth seeing. (I am reminded of the story when King George V, who after having presented Billy Bishop, the first world war Canadian fighter ace with first the Military Cross, then the Distinguished Service Order followed by the Victoria Cross said "Next time you come here Bishop, I will have to make you an Archbishop!"). Yet the mark of the man is that he is as unassuming and modest now as he was all those years ago when he first came to us. His quite remarkable enthusiasm when confronted by a new pupil and his boyish love affair with all things flying and other people's flying is as obvious now as it was when I first met him. We, the Surrey Club and its real successor, the Lasham Gliding Society, have been fantastically lucky in our choice of chief instructors. First Lorne Welch who licked us into shape after the war at Redhill and set the course and direction of the best in British Gliding, then Derek Piggott, surely the outstanding flying instructor of all time, followed by Terry Joint and finally to-day Graham MacAndrew.

Derek has now retired. He has done us proud above and well beyond the call of duty. The Concise Oxford Dictionary defines the 'Hero' thus: "A man of superhuman qualities favoured by the Gods, a demigod, Illustrious warrior".

We dined him out in style at Lasham and the menu serves as a record of some of his achievements. His very talented son Bobby wrote a song at very short notice which followed his father's speech:

He'd like to teach the world to fly in perfect harmony
He'd like to soar in thermals strong, and keep birds company
In loops and stalls and climbing turns he'd lead them through the sky
In anything that flaps or spins, he'd teach the world to fly
From model planes to Optica it matters not to him
But height's important over sea, he doesn't like to swim
On printed page or celluloid he's famous for his grin
But we remember how he looked in Daisy or in Min
If you"ve a triplane or a Spad he'll fly it through a bridge
An airship or a flying boat he'll put it in a ditch
He'd like to teach the world to glide, despite the weather here
You'll hear him in the darkest hour, I think it's going to clear.

The spoof telegrams allegedly sent to him were read out and were greeted with much laughter:

"Darling Derek—I didn't really fancy you until you put my dress on—and then—Wow!"

Signed, Sarah Miles, leading actress, 'Magnificent Men and their Flying Machines.

"Derek—when I got the leading role in the film, I positively refused to fly in that dangerous airship. Bless you Derek for taking my place and thus saving my life. You are the real hero and expert of 'Chitty Chitty Bang Bang'."

Signed, Richard Chamberlain,
Actor.

"Cobber—thanks for teaching me to fly. I am glad you did not take up golf, I reckon you would have beaten me every time."

Signed, Greg Norman, Golfer.

"Piggott, I will always be in your debt. But for you most glider pilots would never have heard of me. Best regards."

Signed, Sir George Cayley, dead Inventor.

"Signor Piggott—Thank God you and I were not alive at the same period of history—no one would have heard of me."

Signed, Giovanni Cassanova, dead roué.

"Derek Piggott—gliding instructor extraordinary. Thanks a million for what you have done for all of us."

Signed, Glider pilots the world over.

Below: Like a 'noble white bird' in mid-flight, with a bewigged Derek Piggott in control of the Cayley
Right: The menu says it all!

THE LASHAM GLIDING SOCIETY

The Dinner and Dance for DEREK PIGGOTT

Menu

Baked Salmon
Gammon Ham
Roast Beef
Coronation Chicken
Green Salad *Coleslaw*
Tomato Salad *Rice Salad*
Kidney Beans and Peppers *Russian Salad*
Roll and Butter
Fresh Fruit Salad in Meringue Nest
Peach and Brandy Gateau
Strawberry Gateau
Coffee and After Dinner Mints

THE SPEECHES

The Master of Ceremonies . . . His Servitude Samuel Mummery BA
The Plauditor . . . . His Eminence Grise Walter Kahn
The Hero of the Hour . . . . the ONLY Derek Piggott
The last Word . . . . His Worship the Chairman of LGS, the Friendly Society, Anthony Mattin

THE BAND

Andy Dickens and the 'Jump, Jive and Wail' Combo

THE ATTIRE

Lounge Suits and /or Dinner Jackets
Dancing Shoes, Woolies and Wellies for the Gentlemen
Anything and Wellies for the Ladies

Trailers at 0100 Sunday 16th April 1989

THE SURREY AND HANTS G C   IMPERIAL COLLEGE OF SCIENCE AND TECHNOLOGY G C   BBC G C   UNIVERSITY OF SURREY G C   IBM G C   ESSO G C   READING UNIVERSITY G C   RICHMOND COLLEGE G C   SOUTHAMPTON UNIVERSITY G C   GUILDFORD COLLEGE OF LAW G C

BOOKS by DEREK PIGGOTT

Gliding (1958)
Beginning Gliding (1975)
Understanding Gliding (1977)
Sub Gravity Sensations and Gliding Accidents (1977)
Delta Papa (1977)
Going Solo (1978)
Understanding Flying Weather (1988)

MOVIES - Pilot and Advisor

Those Magnificent Men and their Flying Machines
The Blue Max
Darling Lili
The Red Baron
Villa Rides
You Can't Win Them All
Chitty Chitty Bang Bang
Guns in the Heather
Chimpmates Airborne
Sir George Cayley, One of Those Magnificent Men
The BBC TV Series "Wings"
Skywards
Slipstream
Agatha, The BBC Hartley Trilogy, a Martini TV Advert, etc, etc.

HIS AWARDS

The Queen's Commendation for Services to ATC Gliding 1953
The Royal Aero Club Bronze Medal 1963
The BGA Diploma for Services to Gliding 1972
Air League of the British Empire Scott Farnie Medal for Air Education 1972
The Royal Aero Club Diploma for Services to Gliding 1987
A member of the British Empire (MBE) for Services to Gliding 1987

TYPES FLOWN BY Derek Piggott

Troop Carrying Gliders

Hotspur, Horsa, Waco CG4a Hadrian

Light Gliders and Sailplanes

Slingsby Cadet, Tutor, T21a, b & C, T31 Tandem Tutor, T38 Grasshopper, Sky, Kite 1, Kite 2, Prefect, Gull 1, Gull 2, Gull 4, Petrel, Eagle, Capstan, Skylark 1, 2, 3s & 4, Dart 15, Dart 17r, T53a & b, Swallow, Swift, Vega, Sport Vega, Olympia 2b, Eon 401, 403, 415, 419, 460, 463, 465, Eton (SG38), Eon Baby, Peak 100, BG100 & 135, Torva, SHK, Blanik, Schleicher K4, K6cr, K6e, K7, K8, ASW12, ASK13, Club Libelle, Hornet, Mosquito, Phoebus, Open Cirrus, Standard Cirrus, Mini-Nimbus, Nimbus 1, Nimbus 2c, Nimbus 3 and 3t, Ventus, Grunau Baby,Kranich 2, Weihe, Minimoa, Rhonsperber, Rhon Buzzard, DG100, 101, 200, 201, Astir CS, Club Astir, Twin Astir, Grob G103, Mucha Standard, Jaskolka, Pirat, Bocian, Foka, Cobra, Jantar Standard, Jantar 1 & 2, Puchacz, Junior, HP14, Schweizer 126, 134, 135, 136, 222, 233, 232, LS1, LS3, LS4, Osprey, Janus B & C, Spatz, Bergfalke 2, 3 & 4, EC2, Canguro, Diamant, Pilatus B4, Fauvel AV36, Kestrel 17 & 19, Kestrel 22, Calif, Bijave, IS28, IS29, IS30, IS32, IS34, Hutter H17, SF27, SF34, Benson Gyro Glider, Lemoine Ascending Parachute, Replica Sir George Cayley's 1853 Glider, M200, Woodstock, TG2, LK Flat Top, Eaglet, Manuel, Pegasus, Pelican, Seviama S-20, Geovier, Falcon 1, AV22, Spyr 5, L0100, Marianne, DG300, IG300, ASW17.

Single Engined

Tiger Moth, PT26 Cornell, Harward, Auster (many variants), Prentice, Spitfire, Balliol, Athena, Chipmunk, Emeraude, Messenger, Victor, Airtourer, Airtrainer, Kittiwake, Super Club (several variants), Pawnee, Cherokee (several variants), Cessnas (150s, 172, 180), Stampe, BA4, Condor, Citabria, Wilga, Helio Courier, B A Swallow, Gipsy 1 Moth, SF260, Stearman PT17, Stinson L5, Jodels (several variants), Beagle Pup, Moth Minor, Falco, Bowkow Junior, Colt, Tri-pacer, Tri-Traveller, Airdale, Husky, Morane 230, Rallye, Provost, Caudron Luciolle, Mooney, Charger, Petrel, Slingsby T67, Fiesler Storch, Decathlon, Robin, Fugi, IS28m3, Jungmann, Caudron C270, Maule, Optica.

Multi-Engined

Oxford, Cessna Crane, Beechcraft Expeditor, Anson, Mosquito, Lancaster, Dakota, Meteor 4 and 7, D H Rapide.

Ultra Lights

Heath Parasol, Motor Tutor, Chilton, Jodel D9, RW3, Tipsy Nipper, Turbulent, Fournier RF3 & 4, RF5a, Southampton University Manpowered Aircraft, Evans VP1.

Microlights

Pipistrelle, Lazair, Shadow, Thruster, Chevron, Pegasus Q.

Motor Gliders

Slingsby T49c, Spatz pv., IS28M1, IS28M2, ASK16, Ogar, PIK 20e, ASK14, Scheibe SF25a, SF25b, c & e Falkes, Tandem Falke, Grob 109a & b, RF5b Sperber, RF4, Milan, DG400, Dimona, Taifun, Janus CM, HB23.

Film Replicas

Bristol Boxkite, Avro Triplane, Eardley Billings, Vickers 22 (Bleriot), Antoinette, Demoiselle, Miles SE5a, Slingsby 7/8ths Mini SE5a, Fokker D7, Fokker Dr1 (Triplane), Phalz, Rumpler, Camel, Albatross DV.

Chapter 14

Retrieves and other stories

In those carefree days of the late '40s and '50s before closed circuit tasks became the norm as the result of higher performance gliders which had better penetration and therefore opened the way to effective crosswind and into wind flying, downwind dashes were the tasks undertaken by pilots. In order to minimise the time delay before the glider was brought back to base so that other pilots could fly, the vital requirement of an efficient crew was all important. To get the best volunteers, pilots were graded by their largesse—cries of "Bloggs is tops, he always buys his crew a four course meal on the way back" or "don't crew for him, he's a mean ...., if you're lucky he might stop for fish and chips" were quite normal. 'UCCs'—utterly committed crews, a term coined for Judy and Brian Slade, one of the very best, honed by Nick Goodhart, polished by Rika Harwood and then inherited by me, were much sought after and worth their weight in gold. When Don Snodgrass, the Chairman of the Southdown Club and a committed bachelor suddenly announced his engagement we asked why. "Damn it, that woman can take corners going round on three wheels when towing and makes fantastic jam butties as well. I can't let her escape".

During competitions the pilot was allowed to return to base for another attempt at the task so it was vital that the crew pick him up as soon as possible after landing and rush back at breakneck speed. Rally drivers do not have better training than we provided. Before two-way radio communication was available in gliders various ploys were used by pilots and crews. As soon as the pilot had set off on the task, the crews would follow and depending on the day and length of task would telephone back to base making a reverse charge call to Control naming their pilot. If nothing had been heard, Control would refuse to accept the charge on the grounds that the named person was not available. When a landing message was finally 'in house' the call was accepted and only then would the crew have to pay for the call. On a good day each crew of the fifty plus gliders taking part might well make ten such calls each and the telephone people got heartily sick of our trick though they never stopped it. It was also very important for the pilot after landing to find a telephone as quickly as possible. Here fitness and stamina were all important as you might have to run some distance to find one. Skilled, clever pilots selected their landing fields not only on size and surface but also in close proximity to a pub, a large country house, a nudist colony (before the 1947 Nationals we had marked all of them on our maps) or at least a farmhouse with telegraph wires going to it.

During one Comps, Ted Stark made a total bog of things and landed only a few miles from the start. The nearest house was across five fields and he set off at high speed. Eventually he reached the last fence and entered the large garden of the house when he saw a deck chair with someone sitting on it. "Have you got a telephone, can I use it?" he shouted whereupon a totally naked nubile young thing leapt up and clutching a large straw hat to her shapely family seat, ran for her life towards the house hotly pursued by a breathless Ted shouting "Stop, I only want to use your 'phone!". She made the house before him and slammed the door in his face. He found a telephone in the village a mile away and by the time his crew found him, he had given up the unequal struggle and after a number of pints of ale lost all interest in flying again that day.

David Ince's wife, Anne, had persuaded her employer Hulton Press to buy the new prototype Slingsby two-seater on condition that the type be called *The Eagle*, the name of their latest children's magazine. A small number of us were invited to fly it providing we were willing to give demonstrations up and down the country. On one of these John Williamson flying with Jim Bunting was forced to land in an unsuitable field in the middle of a large wood. Normally when you landed in a field not in sight of the road, the trick was to tie a piece of coloured cloth to a tree so that the crew would spot it as they reached the landing field. Unfortunately John Willie had forgotten this vital equipment so Jim being ever resourceful climbed a large tree by the side of the road which he reckoned would give him a good view of the oncoming traffic. Suddenly the car and trailer came along at high speed and in an attempt to attract their attention, he threw the only thing to hand which was their 'flying food'—namely a bunch of bananas. The car accelerated and was soon out of sight. When, four hours later, pilots and crew finally met up, John Willie demanded to know why they had not stopped. "Hell's teeth, what would you have done if a bunch of bananas hit the front of your car and up in a tree you saw a large brown object jumping up and down?" was the classic reply.

Finding your glider is one thing, finding your pilot is something else as a

Cambridge club crew discovered. Stuart Waller had completed his Silver 'C' distance by landing on the disused airfield at Ludham which is surrounded by the Norfolk Broads. They arrived at 11 o'clock at night and spent the next hour searching for the Slingsby Prefect and its pilot. Much shouting and flashing the headlights on and off failed to attract their man, when they read the notice in the cockpit which said that Stuart was waiting for them in the local public house. To save time, they de-rigged the glider and in a typical Cambridge bodge managed to stow it into the Skylark trailer they had brought with them. Mine host of 'The Baker's Arms' did not enjoy being woken up at 1am and told them that when the pub closed their man had gone to a bed and breakfast establishment further down the road. "Go away, he's not here—try the local policeman, his house is just down the road" was the irate landlady's instruction shouted to them from a first floor window. In the meantime someone telephoned the police reporting three scruffy suspicious characters seen knocking on doors in the village. Not only did the local bobby appear, but so did two squad cars and a motorcycle cop all of whom eventually believed their story that they were not robbers but merely looking for their pilot. The Law was not impressed, nor were the crew and as it was now after 2 o'clock, they asked the local policeman to tell the missing pilot that he could walk home! When Stuart appeared back in Cambridge that afternoon, he explained that when he was thrown out of the pub at midnight, he found the Church door open, went inside and duly fell asleep.

The variety of landing-out stories is endless and every pilot can tell entertaining and some not so entertaining ones of his own. The subject deserves its own book, so someone ought to start collecting now! Three very different ones prove that a rich vein is waiting to be mined. Strange story—Robin was on a cross-country flight when he found himself rather low over what had been an airfield but was now the site of a large motor car factory. Below him he saw a car being driven round and round a test track and wondered whether the activity might trigger off a nice friendly bubble of warm rising air. The factory makes Japanese cars and the thermal did not materialise. Maybe, he thought, it will be a long flat one instead of a nice vertical one! Very soon he had to land and found some smooth grass near the old runway. He was hardly out of the cockpit when three cars roared up, lots of men jumped out and surrounded him. They demanded his cameras, radios and any other recording devices they insisted he had hidden in his aeroplane. Robin tried to explain, "I'm a glider, no vertical wind, please be careful do not walk on my wings...." but they did not seem to care. Suddenly a black hood was put over his head, he was pushed into a car and driven off. They took him to a room which had no windows and removed the hood. It was only when they started a fierce interrogation demanding to know who he was working for, what had he seen, had he already passed information on to an accomplice, that Robin realised what it was all about. It took him over half an hour to persuade them that his story was true and clinched it by telling them that when his crew came to fetch him, they would see that his car towing the trailer was one of theirs.

"Hello Hello—what's this, engine fell out, did it?" When the arm of the law arrives at a landing site you soon discover whether you have 'Mr. Nice' or 'Mr.Nasty'. Some coppers can be very aggressive, which is not really surprising if they have been out in the fresh air on their bicycles looking for you. But the new breed, like sergeant John Young of the Newbury Hermitage cop shop, who ride around on 1000cc motorbike monsters should be all sweetness and light. Bernard Fitchett, at one stage one of our top young contenders for World Gold, landed in a field near Newbury. He heard the roar of a powerful BMW and soon after saw a figure approaching. Dressed in black leather, black gloves and a black helmet with the visor down over the eyes, the policeman brought out a notebook and pencil and demanded "Name, address, age, occupation, married or single..", Bernard had never been asked such searching questions and the more agitated he became, the worse his speech impediment became which the policeman totally ignored. Just as poor Bernard was close to tears, he was asked whether he had contacted the farmer to apologise for landing unannounced in his field. "Not yet, Officer—I haven't had time, but I will, I promise". "You better laddie, I might want to land here meself" and with that lifted his visor. He had been conned beautifully by John, a gliding friend he had failed to recognise as we tend not to see each other in our working gear!

Landing out can be profitable if you know what you are doing. Frank, who has stopped using his Rolls Royce as his retrieve vehicle, landed one day near a garage. After telephoning back to base, he wandered round aimlessly when he spotted a tree trunk lying behind the garage. Into the garage goes our Frank and starts talking to the owner nonchalantly asking why the tree was lying there. The owner explained that the tree used to stand behind the garage and when he wanted more room he had it cut down. He was going to move it one day when he had time. Frank, who has a large timber company and had recognised the wood, offered to take it away as a favour. The garage owner wouldn't hear of it and insisted that he pay Frank for his trouble. As Frank later admitted—the £25 was a bonus but that tree trunk paid for all his gliding that year!

You will hear stories about cows licking, eating, kicking, jumping over and running round gliders. Bulls also often get a mention but one of the best must be the Chris Rollings, of Booker and BGA fame, and Mike Carlton's epic of wager and gluttony. The whole sordid story entitled 'A load of Bull' appeared in the February 1981 issue of *Sailplane and Gliding*.

Chris on landing in a field had problems with a large brown and white bull which had decided to sample a delicious diet of wood and fabric. Armed with a long stick, he fought hard to deprive the beast of his feast. When his crew who, included Mike Carlton, finally arrived on the scene, the talk was not about the flight but rather about the superb quality of Aberdeen Angus steaks. One thing soon led to another and in no time it was "You couldn't eat a bull that size." "Bet I could." "How long would it take you?" "I'll eat it in a year." "Eat it raw? Bet you couldn't." "Bet I could—in less than a year, and raw." Whether the bet was won or lost, history does not relate. Perhaps we must wait for Chris Rollings's unexpurgated autobiography to find out.

When racing tasks were introduced it was decided to change the take-off order for pilots from the glider competition number sequence to a pilot selected take-off time order. Because you set off as soon as you could after your launch it was important to gauge the optimum time of launch depending on weather conditions. The met. men were in great demand and we hung on their every word of wisdom. Immediately after briefing a large board was set up outside the briefing tent; it had the minutes of the day painted on it, arranged in lines with each minute having its own box complete with a nail. Pilots were issued with discs bearing their competition number and in the selected order of the day would select their time of take-off by hanging their disc in the appropriate box. The pundits played the game relentlessly; if they were at the end of the selection list, they would take a time either well before or long after the main body of competitors, then very obviously be seen to talk earnestly to the met. man, return to the board and change their disc yet again. This always had a greatly unsettling effect on the lesser mortals who would change their discs and place them nearer the great men who would then seize the vacated slot nearer their ideal take-off time! The game sometimes lasted for over an hour, especially if the weather was playing up. If the met. men revised their forecast, bedlam ensued. On one such occasion, as Rika Harwood who was standing in front of the board, disc poised, ready to strike, the mob surged forward and pinned her ample bosom to the nails. Flying that day was delayed as removing Rika resulted in half the nails falling out and after repairing the board, all the pilots had to start all over again.

Groups of friends forming themselves into small syndicates to own a glider was becoming increasingly popular, but early attempts at arranging a fair rota system for flying proved difficult for what was generally a group of rugged individualists. Syndication was said to be more difficult than marriage and often blows were exchanged. In one at Portmoak, things became so fraught that they ended in the Law Courts when one partner welded the doors of the trailer together to stop the other one flying! Another case concerned a syndicate of Royal Air Force officers of which David Innes was a partner, members of the RAFGSA Moonrakers gliding club based at RAF Upavon, a somewhat quaint though very attractive pre-First World War airfield. They owned an SHK sailplane which had a vee tail consisting of two short 'wings'; they found that one partner had removed one of the tailplanes, taken it to the guardroom of their base and ordered the corporal of the guard to lock it in a cell. He further gave the order that no one other than himself was authorised to take it out. When Dimitri Zotov, one the partners found their vital bit, he had to beg the Orderly Officer of the day to countermand the instruction. To avoid a similar thing happening again, they decided to move the glider to another site but as the errant partner was still on the airfield they faced the problem of carrying out the plan without attracting his attention. They found a tug pilot willing to put his career on the line by sneaking out at a very low level until hidden behind the far hills. The tug and glider combination then flew a very large circle to a position east of Upavon until they landed at Thruxton airfield. There Ralph Jones kindly agreed to hide the SHK in his hangar close by. They then flew at this site until the miscreant was very firmly removed from the Air Force and proximity to their machine. Dimitri Zotov hit the National Newspapers some time later, one headline read: 'White Russian New Zealander Royal Air Force pilot flies German glider from Scotland to Ireland!" You can't get more multi-national than that! Now, of course, glider pilots are much more civilised and life is more orderly.

Chapter 15

Pont and Angers

In 1951 the French Air Force invited the Royal Air Force Gliding and Soaring Association to send two pilots to fly at their National Centre at Pont St. Vincent near Nancy in north-east France. In spite of my past misdemeanours, Air Commodore Chris Paul nominated me and a strange young doctor called Brennig James who had recently completed his National Service in the RAF. The stories about this near genius - and you know what some geniuses are—are legion. To his credit is the fact that he started the Thames Valley Gliding Club at Booker airfield near High Wycombe which then was the home of the 'Silver Wings' British Airways Gliding Club created by Peter Hearne, Peter Ross, Roger Neave and others and to-day forms part of the progressive Booker Gliding Club. He has excelled as a soaring pilot, having completed more flights of over 750km than any other British pilot to date. Always full of energy and sometimes crazy ideas he does cause even strong men to wilt and hide in corners when he appears. There is only space for two Brennig stories here, more's the pity. He always arrived at Championships without a crew and press-ganged any unsuspecting bystander to work for him. During one contest he was returning to Lasham after a cross-country flight and was driving along the North Circular Road in London.

Stopped at some traffic lights, some yobs in a car drew up alongside and in next to no time words were exchanged. When the lights turned to green, Brennig, always highly competitive, put his foot hard down on the accelerator determined to show them who was the boss. Some three miles later a car flagged him down and the driver shouted "Mate, something fell out of your box back there". When Brennig and crew stopped and looked into the trailer they found the fuselage missing. As the North Circular Road is dual carriageway, the journey back to find the fuselage was all of five miles. Then to his relief they found the fuselage leaning up against a garden wall totally undamaged. It could only happen to him.

The other story is quite sad in its way. At Pont St.Vincent he was introduced to the French lavatory. For the uninitiated this consists of a hole in the floor with two bars let into the walls on either side at knee height designed to help take the strain of crouching in the very undignified position required. This puzzled the dear boy until we explained that he was supposed to stand on them which he reported as being very difficult. When, many years later he and David Kent took a glider to Nepal hoping to fly over Everest, he was amazed to find the lavatory in his hotel room was of the French variety with the added refinement of a proper loo seat flush with the floor. Not for nothing is he a member of Mensa and he rose to the challenge by sitting on the seat with his legs stretched out. When he pulled the chain, water shot out from under him and flooded his bathroom. The hotelkeeper explained that a European sales representative, a latter day Thomas Crapper, holder of the Royal Warrant, the Order of the Green Cloth, sanitaryware suppliers to her Majesty Queen Victoria, had recently sold them this western refinement which they had just fitted in time for Mr. James's visit. Unfortunately they had not received any instructions and their man had obviously thought that the device should be let into the floor with the seat flush with it.

Pont was great fun. The site is a plateau on a hill but the 'piste' was slightly disconcerting as scattered about in it were small concrete slabs proclaiming 'Ici est mort Monsieur....' The sparse accommodation was in a blockhouse let into the rocks overlooking the valley towards Germany which had been built in the eighteenth century and did not appear to have been touched since. That year the weather was not kind and only flights of one hundred kilometres were possible. We went back there the following year and found the Brits were still regarded with some awe. Nick Goodhart had visited Pont in May 1951, borrowed a glider, and not having a map he unwrapped his sandwiches, traced a few details on to the greaseproof wrapping paper and promptly covered the required three hundred kilometres to secure Gold 'C' No.9 followed later by becoming the first Brit to complete the coveted Diamond 'C'. Rear Admiral HCN Goodhart is a very remarkable man. A naval engineering officer who became a Fleet Air Arm pilot, passed the Empire Test Pilots School course, winner of the World Two-seater Championships flying a Slingsby Eagle in 1956, a contestant in numerous World Contests and winner of the American Soaring Contest. His record breaking flight during a National Championship from Lasham to Portmoak in Scotland still has not been equalled. He invented the mirror landing system for aircraft carriers and was the moving spirit and major force in the design and building of 'Sigma', the variable geometry very high performance sailplane. He then turned his considerable skills to the problems of man-powered flight, designed and built a huge machine which regretfully suffered a mishap in its hangar before full tests could be carried out.

Every morning the 'Chef' would allocate a glider to each pilot and when the great day came he issued his orders. "Petit Distance pour Brevet D (the Silver 'C' fifty kilometre requirement) Messieurs...., Le Grand Distance pour Brevet E (the Gold 'C' distance) Messieurs...... and Le Grand Distance avec But Fixe (Gold distance with a landing at a nominated goal) pour...... "

Five of us, including Brennig, completed the 325km goal flight to Bourges in fine fettle. Then my trouble started. The next Gold 'C' number of the British Register was 10 and as I had landed first I extracted a promise from Brennig that it would be mine. Gliding is a very competitive sport and I just knew that we were both as devious as each other so I telephoned the BGA Office to stake my claim without Brennig knowing. For good measure I also sent off a postcard—just in case! To add insult to injury, that night he and I had to share a single bed. Quite an experience, one which I would not wish on my worst enemy. The next morning the French arranged a twin tow back to Pont. Darling Brennig tried every trick to make me release my rope on the way home in the hope that he would be able to get back to London before me. No chance! I was determined to stay on, come hell or high water.

He had to return by train as 'unfortunately' I had no spare room in my car. Our journey back was horrendous, the poor Vanguard had never been driven so hard. My wife threatened divorce and worse in an effort to get me to reduce speed; I promised ever loving devotion, diamonds, a new kitchen and anything else that came to mind and kept going. Just as Alex, Lady Kinloch, the BGA Secretary, handed me the coveted No.10 badge, the door was nearly torn off its hinges as Brennig shot in shouting 'No.10 is mine'. When he saw us standing there, his face was an absolute picture.

In the sixties the number of British pilots who entered what the French called 'Coupe d'Europe de Vol a Voile, 8 Jours d'Angers' which we immediately renamed 'The Eight Days of Danger' increased substantially. Being French, the competition lasted fifteen days and always started the day after their very special 'Bastille Day' holiday. They are very keen to remember when they stormed the great fortress in Paris at the start of their eighteenth century revolution and so really worked on the Opening Party so that the many pilots from all over Europe should not be left in any doubt of their ability to create mayhem in pint pots. Angers, being in the Anjou wine area of France, provided numerous large barrels of its delectable wine which certainly helped things along. A long trench was dug, filled with charcoal, which was fanned with typical French panache by a parked Stampe tug aircraft, engine running, which was obviously the French equivalent of a ' punka wallah'. All ranks were then issued with metal rods, which had served and probably would again as vital parts of some unknown flying machine. Tubs full of onions, tomatoes, peppers and cubes of meat were provided and when ready you placed your home-made Kebab over the trench and waited until the meat was cooked to your satisfaction. At this point certain foreign pilots who had not been taught to play cricket at school and to whom the concept of fair play was entirely alien came into their own and we found them adept at pinching our skewers which saved them effort and valuable drinking time. On our second visit, we remembered the ploy and brought some really hot chillies with us from the UK which we used to spike our special 'treat' and then waited to see the results—which were very gratifying. Until then, at British National Championships, the Director Ann Welch invariably held back the vital task details until halfway through the briefing when she would hold up a folded cardboard folder and in great dramatic fashion, let it fall open so that the pilots could see the task set. We were delighted that at Angers, the Competition director, Monsieur Herson, who was called 'Le Patron' by one and all, wrote all the details on the hangar door as soon as possible giving full details of the closed circuit tasks including leg distances, headings and other vital information. It thus gave you ample time to work on your maps and when, usually some two hours later, the briefing started, pilots could give their total attention to what was being said. We thought it was a far better system than the one to which we were subjected at home, said so when we returned and luckily the point was taken.

For crews, Angers was sheer bliss. Take-offs were generally after lunch at about 1pm and most finishers came home by six. The crews would launch their pilot, go shopping or sight-seeing and then sit in the swimming pool in the town until their pilot called 'final glide' so that the crew had time to return to the airfield at Avrille. Herson loved his part of France and wanted all of us to see the countryside so deliberately set one task which resulted in out landings. On one occasion as we returned with my glider safely stowed in its box, we came across Humphrey Dimock's trailer sitting by the side of the road with no car in sight. As we walked up to investigate, we heard a strange noise coming from the front. When we opened the door, the sight was hilarious. There was 'Bip Bip' or 'Dimdog' as he was known in the Royal Navy sitting on a make-shift loo. When we pointed out the railway bye-law about waiting until the train had left the station, he replied, "Ah yes, but that only applies in the U.K.!" The 'eight days' were always very enjoyable but keenly fought contests which a number of countries used as their pre-world training and warm-up contest. By the end of the sixties the contest had become the 'de facto' European Championships and in 1973 eighty pilots and gliders from ten different countries competed in the event.

The Stemme S.10, the last glider to carry my competition number

Chapter 16

The Battle for Lasham

The story of the Battle for Lasham should never be forgotten as it does prove that if your cause is Right, you can see off Might! Furthermore I feel it is worth airing my personal opinions as a warning for future generations who might be engaged in a similar endeavour. Great Britain is, of course, the best country in the world. We regard ourselves as highly civilised, justly proud of our method of governing ourselves and indeed have recommended our Parliamentary system to any and all other nations who care to listen. We also felt very safe in our island fortress, the English Channel we regarded as our moat with 'them over there' being strange garlic-eating humans to be kept at arms length. The famous National newspaper headline which proclaimed in large letters "Fog in the Channel, Continent cut off" says it all. We do not have a written Constitution but sometimes do wonder whether Abraham Lincoln's edict of "Government of the people, by the people, and for the people" is uppermost in the minds of some of the elected and non-elected officials who control our destiny.

Until a popular television series called 'Yes, Minister' appeared it was almost certainly true that 'The Great British Public' had no idea of how decisions were made and then carried out. It was claimed that Mrs.Thatcher, the Prime Minister at the time, found the programme compulsive viewing though it is doubtful whether some senior members of the Civil Service were entirely enthralled by the programme's exposé of their methods.

It was also vital to learn and interpret 'Government speak'. When the multitude of civil servants signed their letters with the usual "I remain Sir, Your obedient Servant" you knew it was normal protocol, but when they started with "With great respect", you knew that it meant the exact opposite. Woe betide you if you received a letter which contained both of these phrases as it always rang warning bells that the letter was a real stinker. In our battle to persuade first His Majesty's and then Her Majesty's Government to grant us a lease, we built up quite a collection of them.

Until we started the Battle for Lasham in the early nineteen fifties, we were naïve and wanted to believe that Ministers and their Civil Servants always spoke the truth, wanted the best for all of us and above all were ever approachable. Like children we saw the political world through rose-coloured spectacles. Oh Boy! Were we wrong.

When the Surrey Gliding Club moved to Lasham in August 1951, we were granted a month's security of tenure by the Air Ministry, then the 'owner' of the airfield. This was obviously totally inadequate and after trying to have the term extended without any success, Ann Welch and Hugo Trotter finally demanded and were granted an interview with a senior official. They asked for a twenty year lease and explained that we had great plans for the future, had been asked to hold the National Gliding Championship at the site which could only be undertaken if we had proper security of tenure. The Ministry of Transport and Civil Aviation agreed to sponsor our application but after endless delays the Air Ministry stated that no decision could be made. Repeated attempts to change the official minds over the next two years got us precisely nowhere. When you are confronted by a brick wall, never forget that you can go round it, over it or under it. Furthermore the large number of spiders which had spun their webs in great profusion in the tatty wartime buildings we occupied at Lasham were a constant reminder of the Robert the Bruce dictum 'Try, try and try again!'.

At the Royal Aero Club I had met Squadron Leader (later Air Marshal Sir Peter) Horsley who with Commander Mike Parker was an equerry to his Royal Highness The Duke of Edinburgh. Peter Horsley was the younger brother of Terence who had not only been a pioneering glider pilot but also the Editor of a National Newspaper in the Kemsley group who had persuaded his employer Lord Kemsley to set up 'The Kemsley Trust' which financed most gliding clubs in the U.K. after the war. Over the following months I left lots of gliding literature at Buckingham Palace and was able to discuss our lack of security of tenure problem with his Royal Highness. Not only did he offer to intervene on our behalf but also promised to visit the National Championship which we hoped to stage at Lasham in the near future. You can imagine our reaction when Philip Wills and I were called to Buckingham Palace to be shown a letter from the Air Ministry refusing a lease on the grounds of future possible defence requirements. That all encompassing official phrase was to haunt us for very many years! Now we decided that we had to 'go political' and therefore 'Who you know, not what you know' was the order of the day. During a visit to us at Lasham Peter Thornycroft, then Minister of Civil Aviation, said in his speech 'Dig yourselves in and we will never be able to throw you out!' We took him at his word but it did not get us any closer to being granted a lease.

I noticed that there was a very active Labour member of Parliament called Frank Beswick Having known a Flight Lieutenant Beswick in 2 Group during the war and hoping that he was the very same, I telephoned him at the House of Commons. Although he turned out to be another Flight Lieutenant Beswick, nevertheless he came up trumps, agreed to help and being a member of the Opposition party, liked nothing better than to tweak the Government's tail. Frank Beswick, later Lord Beswick, the Chairman of British Aerospace, arranged a meeting with the junior Minister at the Ministry of Civil Aviation and Hugo Trotter, Frank Irving and I duly went along with him. To this day I still swear that the Minister was either extremely hard of hearing or very tired as for most of the meeting he appeared to have his eyes closed, his mind in neutral and his hearing organs switched to the 'off' position. Surprisingly, however, six months later we were called to a meeting by the Chief Lands Officer at the Air Ministry. He informed us that perhaps a seven year lease could possibly be granted but that we would have to move all our gliders, the clubhouse and workshop to the North side of Beech Avenue, i.e. off the airfield.

Six months of masterly inactivity went by until May 1957 when in reply to questions asked by Sir Roger Conant and Frank Beswick in the House of Commons, Airey Neave, the Joint Parliamentary Secretary to the Ministry of Transport and Civil Aviation spoke at some length about gliding. It will warm the cockles of your heart to read his speech –see 'Hansard' on 21 May 1957 at 23.07 hours, pages 1187-1195. For us the vital paragraph of the speech was "...but my Honourable friend had mentioned Lasham. This is a Royal Air Force airfield and the position at the moment is that the Surrey Gliding Club has been offered a lease by the Air Ministry for quite a substantial period. Negotiations are now proceeding...". We hurriedly formed a Site Committee under the chairmanship of Tony Deane-Drummond who on his appointment to take command of the SAS unit then fighting in Malaya, handed over to Aylett Moore. It was charged to hurry things along and in September 1957 reported that the Air Ministry had decided to release the airfield but had cancelled our promised lease and stopped all further discussion. We now asked the British Gliding Association Council to designate us as 'The National Gliding Centre' in order to give us more clout. After an incredibly acrimonious Council meeting when a certain club north of the Thames objected on the grounds that it would lower its own status, the

Council did eventually agree that Lasham could call itself 'A National Gliding Centre'. We did not think too much of that and indeed in my Appeal letter later on Lasham was described as 'The National and Commonwealth Gliding Centre'. If you are going to put the boot in, do it properly.

In October 1957 the Air Ministry asked all other Ministries whether they wanted Lasham but finding no takers had to offer it back to the previous owner. Some time earlier Commander Marten had fought and won a splendid battle with the Government for ever known as 'The Crichel Down Case' which confirmed that all lands compulsorily purchased during the war must first be offered back to the previous owner when no longer required by the State. As we had always worked hard at being good neighbours, supported the local activities—the Lasham tug-of-war team was in great demand as we invariably lost, our Darts team likewise—so Major Jervoise, the previous owner of the airfield land which is plum in the middle of his extended Herriard Park Estate, very readily agreed that on regaining the freehold he would grant us a twenty-one year lease.

Again nothing happened so we had another question asked in the House of Commons. Then things really started; we discovered that the Air Ministry was applying to the local Council for permission to re-zone Lasham for commercial use which, if granted, would have inflated the value dramatically. Naturally we set to and lobbied all the councillors on the Planning Committee and all other worthies in the area. The application was rejected, we had won that little skirmish. Then the negotiations over price and conditions between the Squire, the Air Ministry and the District Valuer resulted in deadlock and Major Jervoise refused to buy it back at the high price being demanded. Very sadly in May 1959 the Squire died but by his refusal to purchase, the Crichel Down judgement no longer applied and we therefore dreamt up another scheme.

We had created the Lasham Gliding Society for reasons explained elsewhere which, though legally incorporated on 24 December 1958, opened its door to the world on 1 June 1959. Philip Wills in his position as Chairman of the British Gliding Association and the Shaw Slingsby Trust was now asked to join the fray. Philip had far more clout than we could ever hope to muster, his position in the City of London, his great work in the Air Transport Auxiliary followed by a stint in British European Airways, gave him access to most doors.

By November 1960, he reported that the Air Ministry had agreed to sell us the freehold of the whole of Lasham airfield for £70,000 but that ICFC (Industrial and Commercial Finance Corporation) decided that it was only worth £50,000 and would therefore only grant us a mortgage of £25,000 and we would have to find the rest ourselves. The Air Ministry gave us a month to come up with the money but categorically refused to discuss the price question. I immediately launched the Appeal Fund and soon collected £17,000 from our members. However, the deadline passed, ICFC withdrew their promise of funds and with our tails between our legs it was a question of 'back to the drawing board'. In the meantime the first committee and the secretariat of the Lasham Gliding Society had, for various reasons, wound themselves into a small hole and we all decided that it was time for a change. We felt that the new Chairman should not be a member of the old Surrey 'Gang' but be acceptable to the outgoing Committee. We settled on David Carrow who I had first met in Cambridge in 1948 and who had married Barbara, a Surrey member, which we felt made him 'one of us'. We persuaded Philip Wills to wave his old school tie at his fellow Old Harrovian, tell him that it was of national importance that he take the job and thankfully for Lasham he did. History repeated itself many years later when the same ploy was successfully used to persuade David to take on the Vice Chairmanship of the BGA. He had won the Aeronautics Prize at Cambridge, then worked at the Royal Aircraft Establishment Farnborough before joining Lloyd's and becoming a formidable insurance broker. He had also been awarded the Distinguished Flying Cross while a navigator during the war. He brought to the table a keen brain, a fresh outlook to our problem and above all a tremendous keenness to succeed. He and I now started on a never ending round of meetings to try and break the deadlock. Most of the time it felt as if we were running up the down escalator on the underground. There was a dance popular at the time called 'The Hokey Cokey'—you put your left foot in, you pull your left foot out, you put your right foot in and shake it all about... which described the scene very adequately. They would not sell us the airfield so we were going hell for leather for a long lease. The Ministry people would call meetings at which they made sure that we were always outnumbered and during which various ludicrous reasons would be given to explain why they could not grant us a lease.

Two of these particularly spring to mind to show the length officialdom was prepared to go although they must surely have thought things through beforehand. Mustn't they? The first was a classic as they made the mistake, never thereafter repeated, of sending us an agenda which gave us ample warning of what was to come. On the south side of the airfield, the Radio Department of RAE who came to Lasham in about 1953, the same time as Dan-Air the independent charter airline had established their servicing unit in the former Army Club hangar, had established a small enclave round the old control tower. They had recently built an impressive array of aerials some of which were buried in the ground. As these were allegedly so secret and the work of such vital importance, they said that we could not possibly be allowed to operate gliders within miles of them. An agenda item gave enough clues to take prompt action. We rushed Dr. Ken Machin, then the Chairman of the Cambridge University Gliding Club, but more importantly one of the most eminent radio and radar scientists of his day, to Lasham before the meeting for an 'on-site' inspection and evaluation of the endeavour. The meeting started in the usual way—three of us, five of them. "You cannot have a lease because National Security etc etc." But then our 'ringer' demolished all the arguments and proved to them that not only had they got their sums wrong but also the whole of the aerial system was quite useless!. Totally stunned, complete collapse of stout party and the Chairman ended the meeting very smartly.

Another meeting was equally sad though in its own way very funny. The Group Captain commanding Farnborough was wheeled up with six others and had succeeded in wearing David Carrow down with a crazy idea but would not listen to his counter-argument at all. I arrived late as I had been doing battle with some Cubans at their Embassy—real work for David and me had to go on in spite of Lasham which the civil servants realised and played for all they were worth. The faces of the people in the room clearly showed 'stalemate in pint pots'. After a brief resume and on hearing that the latest reason for refusing us a lease was, as the Group Captain explained, in the event of his aircraft suffering radio failure, he would have to instruct them to overfly Lasham on their return to Farnborough. At this point David and I looked at each other and burst out laughing. "Sir" I said, "if the aircraft has suffered radio failure, how will you talk to the pilot?". That too brought the meeting to an abrupt end and back they went to their drawing board.

Would you believe, then, that in May 1962, the Treasury Solicitor sent us a draft lease which, after careful examination, we found to be less than satisfactory. After yet more meetings we were at last able to clear all their various objections and finally on 29 August 1962 we were offered and signed the 'Heads of Agreement'. Victory at last we thought and I set to at once to raise additional funds which we would need to strip and reclad our hangar and build our clubhouse. But even at this late hour our friends thought up yet more devilment. On 28 September the Treasury Solicitor sent yet another letter, this time stating that as the Ministry's examination of the proposed western extension of the London Control Zone indicated a possible effect on all the areas involved, it was premature to complete negotiations with us. In view of this, the Ministry considered that there was no point in sending the linen and paper plans! On 1 August 1962 we had managed to arrange a meeting with the new Parliamentary Under secretary, a gentleman called Basil de Ferranti. Philip Wills, David Carrow and I duly presented ourselves at the House of Commons and no sooner had the meeting started than we realised that the two most senior Civil Servants were (to use a phrase which is now justly renowned having been used by the Head of the Civil Service during the infamous 'Spycatcher' trial) "being economical with the truth". In Cockney rhyming slang—telling 'Porkies'—i.e. pork pies—lies. The Minister angrily refuted our assertions and so, to prove our point, we passed him the damning evidence in the forms of letters signed by the two which they had sent to us. He then made a few ill chosen remarks which he refused to retract before closing the meeting. Philip was horrified and left David and me to cool down. Being young and probably foolish, we decided to give de Ferranti an ultimatum—retract or we will give the story to the National Press. Luckily for us, the day before the deadline was due to expire, the Cuban missile crisis blew up and we realised that the Press would not be too interested in our tale of skullduggery. With hindsight, just as well—you should not really threaten to expose a Minister of the Crown—unless it is a good sex scandal or you are a member of the Opposition party. As history shows, the gentleman in question resigned from the Government soon afterwards, albeit without our help.

We then took counsel's opinion on the matter. Our eminent Queens Counsel stated in his twelve page document dated 1 November 1962 that we had a very strong case to press for a twenty one year lease and in his opinion no Civil Servant would wish to give evidence against us if we went to trial. Part of Paragraph 17 of his opinion is worth quoting in full. "....The political and moral facts are that the Society in establishing itself at Lasham has been carrying out the policy of the Ministry and has acted with the approval and encouragement of the Ministry. Their efforts to establish a gliding centre have been praised and publicised. If there had not been difficulties arising out of RAE's special and independent position, the Lease would have been granted long ago. An attempt by the Ministry to get out of granting the Lease now will surely be regarded, when the facts are known, as DISREPUTABLE AND AS A DEMONSTRATION OF POLITICAL OR DEPARTMENTAL MUDDLE AND INCOMPETENCE...." He finished with, " I believe that the Ministry will be shy of publicity and that "political" action is therefore likely to be effective"".

When we read it, it was champagne all round. Our tails went up like never before! We promptly fired off a letter to the Treasury Solicitor saying that unless a lease was forthcoming within a reasonable period of say fourteen days, we would take legal proceedings to establish our rights. That made us feel much better. Philip Wills then sent a blistering letter to the Minister which would have given any normal human being severe palpitations. The final meeting in this long running saga was held on 15 November 1962 and is very adequately reported in Philip Wills' book, *Free as a Bird.* Philip, David and I, together with Nick Goodhart who we brought along as our Air Traffic Guru, led for Lasham. With our two splendid heavyweight Conservative Members of Parliament, Colonel Freddie Gough, then Chairman of the Royal Aero Club, a veteran of the Arnhem airborne landings and not a man to be trifled with, and our local M.P., the forceful Joan Quennell, we berated Julian Amery, the Minister of Aviation, and demanded that he sign the lease forthwith. After the first hour he called for a short recess. The second hour was almost a rerun of all the meetings we had attended over the past few years, before the Minister said "Yes, maybe!". At that point Freddie Gough went ballistic, threatened to vote against the Government and insisted 'on action this day'. Yet another recess was called and on the return of the Ministerial party, Amery agreed to sign there and then provided that the report not yet written, which he had just instructed the Head of Air Traffic Services to produce examining the effects of future possible requirements in the event of an expansion of Heathrow showed no conflict with our flying, was favourable.

Some months later when the dust had settled, he sent a sweet letter stating that the report showed that there would not be any such conflict! When Amery returned to his office later that day, he is reported as having told his Junior Minister that he had found dealing with Archbishop Makarios during the Cyprus Independence talks far easier than dealing with the those gliders!

It was an historic battle, well worth winning! After yet more meetings we signed a twenty-one year lease with a renewal clause for a further twenty-one year term and included was the all important pre-emption clause which gave us first refusal to buy the freehold if and when the airfield is finally no longer required for defence purposes and is offered for sale. The vital lesson learnt was, in our Democracy, no matter how hard they kick you in the teeth or anywhere else, get up smiling and start again.

The second Battle for Lasham started in 1982 when David Carrow and I met the Ministry people in order to implement the second twenty-one year term of our lease. Although the battle was slightly less acrimonious though just as long-winded as the first one, we had learnt a trick or two from the first battle and won at the end. At the same time we suggested that as the airfield was quite obviously no longer a state asset to be retained in public ownership for 'future defence purposes', they might as well let us buy it. Trying to persuade the Men from the Ministry that bow and arrow production had ceased some centuries before, was a futile exercise and thus we got precisely nowhere as they stood their ground and refused to move.

Many, many meetings followed and at one glorious meeting which John Delafield arranged for us with the top Ministry property man, we were informed that as the work in the black hangar on the south side of the airfield was so very secret, it could not even be discussed. Tony Mattin, the then Chairman of LGS, and I were forced to retire gracefully though not gratefully. Being nosy glider pilots he and I went over to the hangar, found the doors open and a disconsolate gent leaning on his broom. We asked him what he was doing there and he explained that he was a 'resting' actor who had been sent to act as the cleaner by the local Unemployment Office in Alton. He kindly showed us round inside and we much admired sundry old wooden crates, a few beaten up vehicles and various bits of rusting equipment!

In those days the infamous 'D' notice prevented newspapers from publishing 'sensitive' material and the Official Secrets Act was king. At the time of writing, a 'Freedom of Information' Act is being actively discussed, and if adopted and passed by the Government, one wonders what new devilment 'they' will dream up. One day soon I have promised myself a treat, a visit to the Public Record Office at Kew to read all official papers relating to Lasham—it should prove to be most enlightening.

Luckily a good friend of very long standing now came to the aid of the party. He was the Member of Parliament, Sir David Mitchell, then the Minister of State for Transport ,and he agreed to go in to bat on our behalf. With his help, influence and guidance we finally reached an agreement with the Ministry of Defence that we could buy a very long lease on the 284 acres we occupy of the 500 odd acres which make up Lasham airfield. After endless more meetings, we had to settle for a 49 year lease with a renewal option for a further seven year term terminating in 2045 AD for a capital payment of £180,000. The rent thereafter was a notional peppercorn per year—if called for! Just when we thought that we were home and dry, the boys at the Ministry started again.

At this point we asked Bill Walker M.P., a Vice President of the British Gliding Association who acted as the Association's spokesman in the House of Commons, to help by firing a shot across the Minister's bow which he did to great effect. The letter to him dated 17 September 1991 from the Earl of Arran, the Parliamentary Under-Secretary of State for Defence for the Armed Forces, is priceless:

"Dear Bill, Thank you for your letter dated 23 August to Kenneth Carlisle concerning the Lasham Gliding Society's new lease of Lasham airfield from the Ministry of Defence. I am afraid that there has been an inexcusable bureaucratic delay in dealing with this case in the Department. However, I can tell you that the matter has now been sorted out and the agents acting for Lasham Gliding Society are being contacted to complete the transaction. I am very sorry that this problem arose". More champagne! But even then, the Ministry men pricked our balloon just a little—they insisted on back dating the lease to the beginning of 1989. As soon as the ink was dry, we started again—'please, now can we buy the freehold ?'. Patrick Garnett, as Chairman of the Property Committee, who was also the LGS Solicitor and a former Chairman of the Surrey Club and Lasham and I now attended lots and lots of meetings, bent ears wherever we could and kept on and on and on! That little skirmish is still going on but at the time of writing we have reason to believe that we are almost there. Yet again Sir David Mitchell provided the key to the door by introducing me to my incoming local Member of Parliament who was at the time the Minister for Defence Procurement at the Ministry of Defence—the very man who was in charge of our little corner of their empire. The old adage of "Who you know, not what you know" is still true though in modern parlance it is called 'Networking'. Whatever, it works.

A friend has told me that in Ministry circles, the 'Lasham gliders' are considered 'a very determined lot!'

The problem of paying for Lasham is a far less daunting affair than all the years of fighting has been to achieve our goal. In 1982 I started the 'Lasham Trust' and at the same time at last was able to persuade the Committee of the day to institute an airfield purchase fund. Now I have the simple(!) task of inciting our members and friends to donate just half a million pounds which, added to our other funds, will see us home. Fund raising is not much fun, you get brickbats from a few members, mostly the ones who enjoy the fruits of other people's generosity and not often any thanks or appreciation for a task no one else seems to be willing to undertake. However, when our goal is achieved, I promise not to ask for any more donations ever—and to die happy!

'...brother can you spare a dime— or two?,

LASHAM GLIDING SOCIETY LTD

Registered under the Industrial and Provident Societies Act, 1893, on 24 Dec, 1958, No. 15094 R. Hants.

LASHAM GLIDING CENTRE ALTON HANTS

Telephone: HERRIARD 270

COMMITTEE OF MANAGEMENT

D. D. Carrow DFC MA (Chairman)
Lt. Col. Sir Charles Dorman Bt. MC MA (Vice-Chairman)
M. Gee MA FCA
F. G. Irving M.Eng DIC AFRAES
W. A. H. Kahn
P. Minton B.Sc(Eng) ACGI
C. J. Sellick MA
J. Simpson MA
J. N. Cochrane BA (General Manager)

March 1962

An appeal for the National and Commonwealth Gliding Centre

Since the war British glider pilots and British gliders and ancillary equipment have been the most consistently successful in World Championships. Our pilots and machines have won first and second places more often than those of any other nation. We are today the largest exporters of high-performance machines in the world and have sold gliders to every continent. The only British-designed and British-built aircraft sold to Russia since the war have been gliders.

Although this is extremely satisfactory, we lack a National Centre where our methods and techniques can be taught not only to a greater number of our own pilots, but also to pilots from abroad who will then buy our equipment for use in their own countries. All the Iron Curtain countries and most other European nations have established such centres, and we are in danger of losing our markets and the leading position in our sport.

Unlike countries abroad, we are not subsidized by our Government. We do not want a subsidy, since we value our independence. The British Gliding Association manages and regulates gliding without cost to the taxpayer, and our record of safety and competence is the best in the world.

The National and Commonwealth Centre is now being established at Lasham Gliding Centre. Lasham is a wartime aerodrome situated between Alton and Basingstoke in North-east Hampshire. The eight hundred members of the eight clubs which operate at Lasham have formed a Friendly Society called the Lasham Gliding Society, and this co-ordinates all flying, provides all facilities and employs the permanent staff. It is administered by a Committee of Management whose elected members are the senior members of the clubs and whose secretary is the full-time general manager.

After eleven years of uncertainty owing to lack of security of tenure, the Society has been granted a 21-year lease (with an option to renew for a further term of 21 years) by the Ministry of Aviation.

To date we have had to make do with unsatisfactory buildings erected during the war; these reached the end of their useful life some time ago and we must now demolish them and rebuild. Our three vital needs are a hangar, workshops and a living block comprising bedrooms, lecture rooms, restaurant, bar and offices. A start has been made on the hangar, as we could not protect our equipment in the dangerous and leaking old hangar for yet another winter.

All this is costing a great deal of money—in fact we need £40,000. An appeal to our members has produced gifts of over £17,500 so far and I am confident of raising £20,000 from them when they have all contributed. May I ask you to help us to achieve our goal? We have helped ourselves to the best of our ability but are now facing the problem of raising the difference. Although we could raise a loan we feel that this would be imprudent, as it would saddle us with a large repayment problem which would undoubtedly raise the cost of gliding and thus defeat our object.

We earnestly believe that our efforts at Lasham are really valuable to the well-being and prosperity of this country.

"*. . . The air has come of age in this half-century with a burst of energy and momentum of development. I do not believe this momentum will be allowed to flag in other countries and we must not let it flag in ours either.*

"*Our young men must be convinced that in the air lies real adventure, interest and reward. . . .*"

Lord Mountbatten, December 16, 1961.

Please do help us so that we can help others—we shall be most grateful. May I ask you to send any donations to me at the address above. If I can give you any further information, please ring me at my London office, telephone number FLEET STREET 5751, and I will willingly come and see you.

Yours sincerely,

WALTER A. H. KAHN,
Chairman, Appeal Committee, Lasham Gliding Society Ltd

Chapter 17

Fund raising and Downbeat

With the signing of our lease in 1962, re-cladding the hangar to make it safe was our first priority, to be followed by building a new clubhouse worthy of 'The Gliding Centre'. As parts of the roof of the hangar kept falling off, we stored all the gliders in the other large T.2. sited in the field north of Beech Avenue. Every day at the start of gliding and at the end of the day we moved everything across the road on to and back from the airfield. Neither our members nor the traffic using the Avenue were too happy with this arrangement.

An appeal letter was produced, I signed seven thousand of them personally (never again) which were sent to our members and friends and I set out to canvass possible donors up and down the land. Unfortunately for us, Brigadier George Chatterton, the former Commanding Officer of the Glider Pilot Regiment, ably supported by Sir Fredrick Hoare, the immediate past Lord Mayor of London, was also raising funds for his 'Upward Bound Trust' which to this day provides gliding training at Thame airfield near Aylesbury for youngsters in memory of those who flew gliders during the war. He and I met very often going into or coming out from the offices of likely sponsors.

Sometimes in life, ripe apples do fall off trees at the most opportune moment. On 16 December 1961, at the annual Air League lunch, the guest of honour, Admiral Lord Mountbatten, finished his speech with these stirring words, "The air has come of age in this half century with a burst of energy and momentum of development. I do not believe this momentum will be allowed to flag in other countries and we must not let it flag in ours either. Our young men must be convinced that in the air lies real adventure, interest and reward...". It was obviously tailor made for our appeal and having quite innocently used the splendid quote from his speech in the appeal letter, I was ordered to his office to be given a monumental rocket by him. "How dare you, don't you know that you are not supposed to use any statements made by Royalty without prior permission! You will go to the Palace and explain that you failed to ask, you will apologise and return to me when you have done so!" he thundered. For once I kept silent and did not explain that I was not aware of his Royal status. When Commander Mike Parker ushered me into HRH the Duke of Edinburgh's room to make my abject apology, my appeal efforts were immediately rewarded. Writing out a cheque, he handed it to me with the instruction to show it to his Uncle as proof of the apology and suggested that I might even be given a donation by the Admiral. My return visit was happier than the first, after which he sent me a gracious letter hand written in green ink accepting my apology—but sadly no cheque.

Kenneth MacAlpine of the famous building and construction family agreed to design and build our clubhouse and so one day I was despatched in an Auster to Luton Airport to fly an architect and his wife to Lasham for a site inspection. On arrival, as I had no idea what he looked like, I went to the information desk and explained my problem. "That's easy, I'll announce your arrival, call for your man and then announce your departure" said the helpful lady. Over the public address system, the waiting bucket and spade brigade heard "Lasham Airways announce the arrival of flight No.1 from Lasham. Will passengers please proceed to Gate No.3. Lasham Airways Flight No.2 to Lasham will depart in fifteen minutes". The faces of the holidaymakers as we climbed into the Auster parked next to various airliners was a classic and made it a day to remember. He designed a beautiful two storey clubhouse but well beyond our meagre means. Happily a club member called Robin Cole came up trumps and let us buy the prototype of his revolutionary 'Kingsworthy' building for an absolute snip. It is of interest that the Dunstable clubhouse designed by Kit Nicholson and our Lasham 'Condor' building both won design awards in their day, though it must be admitted that theirs is attractive whereas ours is purely functional.

We had collected just enough money to reclad the hangar and build the clubhouse but with nothing left over for the internal fittings and fixtures. Frank Kinder, an architect member, designed the interior but we had a major shortfall. The problem was soon solved by a chance meeting with a Director of British European Airways. Over lunch at the Royal Aero Club I timidly asked what they intended to do with the contents of their West London Terminal which was being replaced by a new ten storey one in Cromwell Road in London. I explained our needs and one week later the Board agreed to let us tender for all the kitchen equipment, the complete bar and cafeteria complete with tables and chairs. A figure was agreed but at that moment we still did not have a bean! Lady Luck in the guise of

Wladek 'Rad' Radwanski smiled on us. He was a great man then running a restaurant in the City of London which was one of my favourite lunchtime haunts. He had studied Law at Warsaw University but realising that war was fairly imminent persuaded his father to let him transfer to the Polish Air Force. He achieved his ambition to become a fighter pilot, then a test pilot and when Poland fell, fled first to France and then to England. He joined the Air Transport Auxiliary ferrying a variety of aircraft to squadrons around the country. Philip Wills, then second in command of ATA, remembers 'Rad' as the member of a very select team of pilots used for the most dangerous urgent flights carried out in very unsuitable weather. Before the end of the war 'Rad' managed to transfer to the RAF and joined Bomber Command. When he was demobilised, not wishing to return to Russian occupied Poland, he found himself at a loose end with no prospects, money or job. While at university, the students had rebelled at the low quality of the food in their canteen and 'Rad' found himself in charge of the kitchens. So now he decided on catering, started as a waiter, saved his money and eventually bought 'The Charterhouse' in Charterhouse Square. When I first met him, he was sad and lost due to a personal bereavement and we talked flying endlessly. When the Lasham shortfall problem was explained, he readily agreed to give us the required amount on condition that he could have any surplus equipment for a derelict hotel he was refurbishing at Salfords in Surrey. Later to help Poland's economy, he started 'Anglo Polish Sailplanes' and importing gliders for sale in the United Kingdom.

So 'Operation Downbeat', our code name standing for 'Demolition of West London British European Airways Terminal' was set in motion. We realised that we would have to work fast as some of the demolition crew had ideas not dissimilar from ours. On a Wednesday at six in the evening we hit the building like a plague of locusts and set to with a will which surprised everyone. By the next evening, the kitchen, cafeteria and bar were stripped bare and our goodies safely stored off the site under lock and key. The rest of the building proved very inviting and the arrival and departure desks looked very tempting, as did light fittings, door stops, fire hoses and many other desirable objects. The Lasham Air Scouts had their eyes on the wooden floor tiles and some wash basins, and a metal grille in front of the bookshop was just what we needed for our bar. A quick decision had to be made and as my remit was only to take what was agreed, the others banished me to what had been the bar, there to act as 'Camp Clearance Officer' to whom they would come for permission to 'liberate' whatever took their fancy. They never did and my conscience therefore was almost clear! "If we took it," I said to myself, "it would go to a good cause. If we did not, it would probably be taken and sold with the cash going to someone who did not have the same high ideals as we had". At least that was the speech I was mentally preparing to give from the dock if..... All was well until I was sent for by the Station Manager who was livid because someone had broken into his 'private' store and removed various items. Just as he was demanding that we return everything, I saw a crocodile of small Air Scouts emerge from one door carrying a set of ten wash basins all still connected together with their hot and cold copper pipes. To save the day and to prevent him seeing this remarkable spectacle, I grabbed him by his lapels, put my face very close to his and started an animated diatribe on the unfairness of his allegations until I saw the crocodile disappear through another door. He went off, totally puzzled but did not trouble us again. Some of the basins can still be seen in the Vintage Glider Club building at Lasham. As we worked from six in the evening until midnight, we were all getting very tired. Two Security Guards who were watching two worn-out young Imperial College students sawing up a highly desirable departure desk with a two handed saw, took pity on them, told them to have a rest while they carried on until their bossman arrived unexpectedly. By Saturday evening we had finished. All our goodies we had moved in glider trailers to a temporary safe storage building out of sight of prying eyes.

After we had taken our pick—the office hatch desk and a few light fittings in the Lasham clubhouse survive to this day—we sold various items to other clubs which did wonders for our finances. The only money we had to spend on equipping our new clubhouse was under three pounds for notice boards green baize. By dint of Frank Irving's standing as a very senior lecturer in Aeronautics at the Imperial College of Science and Technology, we were given permission to store our goodies for a very short time in an adjacent building to the College. Our Aladdin's cave was on the ground floor of the imposing structure now in the middle of the Imperial College complex in South Kensington known as the Imperial Institute Tower much loved by Sir John Betjeman who successfully lobbied Parliament to save it for the Nation. As the preservation works were due to start on the following Wednesday, there was no time for us to collect the remainder of the desks, firehoses and reels, and light fittings stored there. In order to stabilise the building, concrete was pumped into the first and second floors of the tower. When eventually the tower is finally demolished, people will be very surprised when our surplus embedded in concrete comes to light. After we left at six in the evening for a well deserved pint or two, an upper floor of the new terminal building caught fire at 2 o'clock the next morning! When my chum telephoned the Chairman of the Airline to give him the news, the Chairman said "Right, transfer back to the old building, ready for our passengers in the morning". When Ian replied, " Sorry, not possible, the gliders have stripped it bare" there was a pause followed by the classic reply from the great and noble Lord, "The bastards, have they now!".

A Winter Night at Lasham
Words by R.P.

A swarthy, bulky Lashamite, creeping through the dark
He says he's got up early, to D.I. a Skylark
But we know better—this blackguard can't D.I.
He's our resident fund raiser, surveying the Southern sky
The time is just five thirty—'twill soon be morning light
He hears a plane approaching—a droning in the night
It's the Rapide—fully laden, with smuggled precious stones
It lands upon the runway.
The cold wind bites his bones
A sack is thrown out to him—the Rapide roars away
Its destination, Ireland.
Before the break of day
As dawn creeps o'er the pylon our hero trudges back
It's for the cause of gliding that he lugs that precious sack
His actions may be risky, but he's a clever boy
His mission is for gliding—in comfort and joy
He thinks not of the diamonds that his smuggled prize contains
But toilets, a clubhouse, and miles of luverly drains
This is but one example of what our members try
In order to ensure that 'The Hub' will never die
Pray join me in a toast—To Wally and his gang
Their efforts won us Lasham.
A place to fly—and prang!

Chapter 18

Wills, the World Champs and the Irish

As Chairman of the BGA Development Committee, it was my duty to squeeze money out of the Department of Education and quite a number of clubs were able to buy gliders, winches and other equipment as the result of dipping into the public purse. In late 1963 the policy changed and our source of funds dried up abruptly. One evening in November after a particularly festive Tobacco Trade Dinner, a crowd of us finished up in the W.D.& H.O.Wills hospitality suite at the Dorchester Hotel. During the banter that followed, John Wilson, then the Marketing Director of the company, boasted that Wills were the major sponsors of sport in the U.K. Quick as a flash I bet him that my sport was not on his list and added that if I was proved correct he would have to agree to help us. Gliding won and the Wills (Philip Wills was not a relation of the great tobacco family from Dulverton) largesse thereafter knew no bounds. Numerous flying scholarships were followed by an imaginative competition for club nominated pilots who were put through a very fierce test of their gliding skills and technical knowledge with one northern and one southern region winner each to take a shiny new Slingsby T.49 two-seater to be donated to their respective clubs. Two Ultra radios and two Winter barographs were given to the 2nd and 3rd best pilots. Fred Slingsby agreed to the name 'Capstan', so called after a leading Wills cigarette brand of the day, to be the designated name for his new T.49 side by side training machine. The first production glider Wills donated to the BGA to be used by the National Coach. Unfortunately the Capstans were not finished in time for the 'Wills Challenge' so two K.6 single seaters were given as the major prizes. They were much appreciated by the winning clubs and, for the record, do read the report in the October/November 1968 edition of *Sailplane and Gliding* written by a sweet modest young blonde girl called Gillian Howe who proudly took a K.6 back to the Cotswold Club at Aston Down. Thirty years on, she is still as pretty as she was then as her photograph in S & G will confirm! Fame brings its own reward and she was offered a job in the BGA office where she met another young pilot called Justin Wills. For years now she has emulated her famous mother-in-law, Kitty Wills, by chasing after her husband for more miles in different countries of the world than most wives have ever done.

More Wills sponsorship competitions followed and by the time W.D. & H.O.Wills moved on to newer money-hungry spectator sports such as Formula One motor racing, they had given us nearly One Million Pounds in today's money. As Britain was chosen to host the 1965 World Gliding Championship, Wills really came up smelling of roses and promised to underwrite the whole cost of the enterprise. Their financial aid and media expertise made the event held at South Cerney near Cirencester a great success. The weather was not too kind and the foreigners found flying over England rather difficult but a great time was had by all.

The Irish Gliding Association decided to enter a team for the very first time and invited Paddy Kearon to be their senior pilot. Paddy was a truly tremendous human being. I make no apology for my obvious hero worship —my generation was brought up to revere and respect great men of whom there were still a large number (do I hear "unlike to-day"?). It is a sad reflection of our time that now when most young people are asked to name just one or two of their personal heroes, they seem to have considerable trouble to think of any, let alone ones who are still alive to-day and who they might even have met. Norman Walter 'Paddy' Kearon was and always will be one of my special heroes and of all the thousands of glider pilots I have met, he was the nicest, the kindest and the best friend of all.

Born in Dublin, Paddy came from a long line of Wicklow seafarers. An outstanding athlete, he just missed being selected to run for Ireland in the 1936 Olympics but, on coming to England, represented the London Metropolitan Police in various National and International races as a superb miler. He joined the RAF in 1939 and although an Equipment Officer was mentioned in despatches no less than five times. We first met in 1945 when Paddy was one of the many Wing Commanders (we decided the collective noun for them was 'a flush of W/Cs') who started gliding at Salzgitter and Oerlinghausen.

He was a typical great Irishman who had a tremendous sense of humour and a total lack of pretentiousness; the ability to make endless pints of Guinness disappear which always made me wonder why the Liffey ever had any water flowing through Dublin's fair city; and an ever open helping hand for anyone in need. The RAF Gliding Centre at Bicester which he was mainly instrumental in creating, the battles to protect Andy Gough the Chief Instructor and other servicemen who he 'lost' from other duties and his continual successes in acquiring gliders and equipment are all testimonies to his dedication to our sport. There is no doubt that without him RAF Gliding would have withered and died and moreover his perpetual fight to further the interests of service gliding did not endear him to his Lords and Masters. But for that, although he retired as an Air Commodore, he would undoubtedly have reached even higher rank.

Captain Kelly Rogers, the most famous of all Irish flying pioneers, was the prime mover of the Irish entry. Paddy asked me to be the Team Manager explaining that with an émigré Irishman serving in the British Royal Air Force as one pilot, a New Zealander called Tom Evans, an Aer Lingus pilot with an Irish wife as another and an English tax exile called Mike Slazenger of the tennis equipment family as the third, he felt that as my wife's mother had been born a Doran in Dublin, my inclusion in the team made it almost respectably Irish.

When Paddy and I flew over to be instructed by Captain Kelly Rogers to "put Ireland on the gliding map, even if you don't win" we knew what we had to do. As he had arranged for us to be interviewed on Irish television by a formidable lady called Petronella O'Flanagan who was as large as she was fierce, he decided that I should have an Irish name and from that moment on was no longer Wally Kahn but Seamus O'Caihan. After the interview Petronella invited us to dinner at the Dolphin Hotel, then owned by Ma Nugent whose late husband had been my family company's Irish agent for very many years. The Dolphin was a wonderful watering hole much frequented by the horse-racing and arty fraternity. Ma and Petronella entertained us in such great style that when at last we were poured out of the place in the early hours, neither of us could remember the name let alone the location of our hotel. We wandered the streets of Dublin until we found a house offering bed and breakfast. Being knocked up by two drunks in the early hours of the morning did not seem to worry the owner at all, in fact he was probably quite used to it. He showed us into a downstairs room which had two fairly rudimentary beds on one side and the biggest wedding cake I have ever seen on the floor on the other side. We were made to swear on the Holy Bible that we would not touch the cake and at last fell asleep. After what was probably only about two hours we were woken up by an enormous commotion and confronted by a large and very irate female who accused us of peeing on her daughter's wedding cake. As neither of us had any recollections of what we might have done during the night and were desperately trying to think of plausible denials, the large scruffy family dog came to our rescue. It walked into the room, went straight over to the cake and lifted its leg. Quick as a flash Paddy said, "Sure, I remember now, the beast came in during the night". The dog got his own back by leaving us some of his fleas—and to think we paid all of five shillings for the privilege.

At the World Champs we Irish decided to show the world a thing or two. Paddy organised the biggest radio truck fully equipped with HF and VHF radios. Our aerial array was so high and impressive that the organisers gave us a hard time as other teams suspected us of using some new and illegal technology. The fact that some American pilots were using VOR beacons for navigating which was strictly against the rules did not make our life any easier. At the opening ceremony all the teams were lined up in front of their national flags. It was a very cold day and we all froze during the carefully scripted ' short' speech by Roy Jenkins, now Lord Jenkins of Hillhead, then the Minister of Aviation. Philip Wills as Chairman of the BGA and Ann Welch the Director of the Championships then introduced the Minister to each team in turn. With Captain Kelly Rogers' instructions ringing in my ears, I had dreamt up a fiendish plot to give the Press photographers a great photo-call opportunity and also produce good copy. My Lord Jenkins is renowned for his great love of fine Claret and I thought that he ought to sample some good Irish Whiskey, which later he admitted was to be the first and probably the last time in his life. A friend at Allied Breweries had given me an ample supply of cardboard cups which advertised the 'Double Diamond' brand of beer. Being only a temporary Irishman I failed to realise the explosive significance of the 'Double Diamond' logo which was a red hand! When the Minister reached us, I asked whether he was as cold as us and promptly pressed a paper cup in his hand, produced the Whiskey and gave him a generous Irish measure of three fingers albeit vertical rather than horizontal. Every time he tried to take a sip, he was introduced to another team member which gave my Press friends ample opportunity to get all the shots they wanted. At last Philip said that they must move on, so I turned the Minister round to face the press, gave him the Irish toast and suggested he knock his drink back in one. His face was a picture. Photographs of Roy Jenkins holding the cup were published in newspapers in fourteen different countries and our friends back in Dublin were delighted. Whether the cup with the Red Hand of Ulster on it was a diplomatic thing to do is open to doubt in view of the later sad events in Northern Ireland.

Every country was asked to host a party restricted to the pilots and their team managers. Each offered their native brand of fire water—the Americans had gallons of Bourbon, the Russians Vodka, the Yugoslavs produced Slivovitz and so on. We had only been able to scrounge a dozen bottles of Irish Whiskey which was obviously not enough for what we had in mind. On a non-flying day we rushed down to Somerset and collected one hundred gallons of the strongest scrumpy we could find and then announced that the Irish team cordially invited everybody at South Cerney to their party. The effect was electric, the result dramatic. Very few of our guests had ever sampled what we said was Irish Country Cider. The particular scrumpy we served was the unfiltered kind with a kick like a mule and no one had ever managed more than three pints. After an hour, bodies out to the world were lying about all over the place. At one stage the Assistant Russian Air Attaché, Colonel Valentin Elistratov thanked me warmly for inviting him, expressed the opinion that "Your Irish cider not very strong" and promptly passed out at my feet. The next morning when the cleaners arrived to prepare the corner of the hangar we used for the morning briefing, they found over thirty people still fast asleep on the floor.

When after the farewell banquet and presentation of the prizes, the report in *Sailplane and Gliding* stated "All were cheered, the loudest cheer going to the Irish and the longest to the Russians". When we reported back to Captain Kelly Rogers he said "Well done boys, you didn't win but begorrah, they knew you were there!".

'Your health, Minister'

Chapter 19

We have 'em, even if they are not all there

No one book can hope to do justice to the rugged individualists who glide; their idiosyncrasies, their numerous stories and above all their strange and odd antics. At the time of writing, having 'glided', 'glid', 'glud' or whatever you call it, for fifty-four years without a break, I can only try to offer the reader a small selection to prove, though loveable—we are an odd lot! We come in all shapes and sizes, from dukes to dustmen and only severe mental disability prevents us from flying. Physical disadvantage is no bar, we have blind as well as deaf pilots, those who have only one leg—the great pilot and designer Wolf Hirth had a wooden leg which is why he fitted hinges to the bottom of the rudder pedals of his gliders, and others who suffer from more extreme problems. Mental problems of the thought process variety are less easily discernible. At Lasham we have two members known as 'Evans the elevator' and 'Evans the rudder'. The former is our presiding genius running the restaurant which provides fantastic food seemingly at all hours of the day, though how he acquired his nickname is his story which, if pressed, he will tell you. The latter is remembered for the occasion when the rudder of his Kestrel fell off just after he had released from the tug at 2000 feet. After careful consideration he decided to abandon ship but he remembered Derek Piggott's story of how he once told a pupil to bail out, but the student dithered and when Derek asked him why, after they were safely on the ground, the student said he was putting his sunglasses away!". 'Evans the rudder' had just bought a pair of very expensive prescription varifocal photochromic glasses which he feared would blow away if he jumped, so, being a former member of the Cambridge club he quickly analysed the problem, very carefully put them safely in the pocket of the glider and then jumped. For a minute after jumping out, he wondered if he had done the right thing, the glider as gliders will, seemed to be flying better without him and it struck him that he knew little about his parachute which the syndicate had just bought off another member. All went well, he was relatively undamaged as indeed apart from one wing was the Kestrel which came to earth quite near him. The glasses also came down, still in the fuselage, and were totally undamaged. John D'Arcy from whom they had bought the parachute had the last word "You're not very trusting are you? Got to test my 'chute' to make sure it works!".

Jumping out of gliders is not really something which anyone enjoys at the best of times but when things fall off your pride and joy, you have to take to the silk. One of our more adventurous Imperial College Club members was a very lucky little man. He had climbed in their club's Skylark 4 to 7,000 feet in cloud when it all turned to a can of worms. The speed built up alarmingly and sadly he failed to open his speed limiting dive brakes which would have solved his problems. The Skylark broke up, the fuselage split open like a pea pod and he found himself falling out downwards. He was so lucky, no part of the glider snagged his parachute and he floated gently to the ground. In point of fact, when the wreckage was examined, all the bits were found except the torque tube. An RAF helicopter from Odiham happened to be flying in the area, the crew watched and enthralled by the event, landed next to him in the field and took him back to their base. The glider pilot was not impressed or even very concerned by his lucky escape. Before he left, never to be seen again, he explained that as a trained parachutist it was just another jump!

The next story concerns a gentleman from 'up north'.

Our Club's the Yorkshire Club

To be sung to the tune of 'My girl's a Yorkshire Girl'

Our Club's the Yorkshire Club
Yorkshire through and through
Our Club's a right good Club
Eh, by gum, it's champion
'Sling's' got his works quite near
And lent us all his stuff
We chuck 'em about as soon as we get 'em
For we take some beating.
We're tough.

For good order and discipline and wanting to make certain that my memory was not playing tricks, I wrote to a certain renowned member of the Yorkshire club who figures in this 'Northern Saga of yesteryear': "Back in the 50's, or was it in the 60's, one of your members carried out a most interesting flight. You described him as a terribly nice, well brought up gentleman—although just a little vague! Please can you verify the story for me as I would like to use it". After a total silence and nil response, a telephone call to him confirmed my worst suspicions. He could not really remember the details but he was sure that I had muddled up two different flights. *C'est tout*—no more. Full stop. Collapse of stout party but to hell with it. Publish and be damned! Here it is:

Came the day when the proper gent decided to fly south from their Sutton Bank site in order to complete his Silver 'C' distance. The wind was right, the sky showed promise of lots of lovely white fluffy cumulus clouds and it had the makings of a classic 'barn door' day. Off he went in his Skylark full of the joys of spring and like the song said "... and the three little fishes swam and swam right over the dam". With the landscape underneath him changing apace, our hero thought 'things are really going well, soon I will be miles away, maybe I should keep going on and on, I might then get my Gold 'C' Distance as well!'. On and on he flew, hour after hour, not having a clue of how far he had flown or for that matter where he was. Sitting there, munching a bar of chocolate, he tried to visualise his possible route. 'Keep heading south and when the sea comes into view, turn west and head for Cornwall'. Easy really when you are a pundit but then a horrible thought struck him. Down south, on track, will be London Heathrow Airport. Have to avoid that! Just then, he suddenly saw a big, big aeroplane. It had windows all along the fuselage and as he watched he saw the wheels coming down. There in the distance was this huge airfield and HIS aeroplane was going down to land there. 'Heathrow—heavens, they must have seen me, what shall I do—best thing follow him, land there as well, apologise and all will be well'. So he followed HIS airliner down.

To the side of the long runway he saw a big building with a lovely grass area in front of it which looked like the perfect landing spot. His landing was textbook and as he opened the canopy he heard clapping and cheering. On the building were lots of people and they were applauding him. He felt good, climbed out and bowed to them. They cheered and clapped again, so he bowed again and just then two large men drove up in a car. "I say you chaps, could you look after my glider, I just want to find a telephone". "Come with us" they said. "No one will come near your glider—we've been ordered to take you to Administration".

He was propelled along endless corridors and then pushed through a door marked 'Commandant' and saw him sitting behind a large desk. "I say, you are Skeffington Minor (obviously I have changed the name), I have not seen you since our school days—Gosh! you have done well for yourself —Commandant of Heathrow, who would have thought it". "You haven't changed since school, you're still a twit" he replied "and what's more I am not the Commandant of Heathrow, I am the Commandant of Birmingham Airport! What the blazes are you going here?". So our hero explained—how sad, he had completed the Silver 'C' distance but had missed the Gold 'C' distance. Now he would like to telephone the club, get someone to fly down and aero-tow him home. "Aero-tow you home, from here! What are you talking about, don't you chaps have trailers?". "True, we do. But I have promised my wife that I would be back for dinner to-night. So please Skeffington, for old time's sake, just this once".

The Yorkshire Club Elder was walking past the telephone in the round clubhouse when he heard a member shout into the telephone "You landed where, Birmingham Airport? You want an aero-tow?". The Elder snatched the 'phone from his hand and said " Shut up, just answer Yes or No to my questions, whoever you are" but before he could go on he was interrupted "Ah, it's you.....,old boy. Come and fetch me with the Auster, it's all right, I've got permission from the Commandant, we were at school together. Here I'll put him on the line". Arrangements were made, information exchanged and future warnings given. Our hero explained that as he would have to wait for an hour or two until the tug arrived, he might as well invite the Commandant to a late lunch and suggested that a good bottle of claret would help his digestion. The offer was declined!

The Tug duly arrived and off they went. Just over Silver 'C' distance away—on track is East Midlands airport. Lucky really because that is where they ran out of fuel and had to land. The pity was that the Commandant there did not go to school with either of them! The other great pity is that 'The Elder' cannot remember the story! All that happened a long time ago and would certainly not occur to-day. Glider pilots take great care not to infringe airspace closed to them and keep a long way from the special areas which surround civilian and military airfields. Not only do they always carry the very latest air maps but with the Global Position System Instruments, they are able to pinpoint their exact location and height at all times. The modern pilot is very disciplined and conscious of the freedoms we enjoy and treasure.

"Please, Mister, can we have another ball please!". This story concerns two well to do gents who bought themselves a new French 'Pegase' single seater and thought it fun to have it aero-towed back to Lasham. None of the Lasham tug pilots wanted the task as we were not sure that the new owners were up to the long tow back from the factory at Le Blanc. Bob Bickers, being made of sterner stuff, agreed and so the three pressed off in Bob's Rallye Commodore. Both pilots had one flight at Le Blanc to learn how to fly their new toy and mindful of their comfort, Bob used a 300 foot towrope as he thought that it would give them a smoother ride. The plot for the next day was to tow to Le Touquet on the French coast, have a little rest, swap pilots in the glider and then press on home. Bob now takes up the story:

"The day came and was obviously going to brew into at least a 500km day and it was really delightful to be alive. After ten minutes we had reached 2000 feet and had more or less settled down. We then went through a strong thermal, a few moments later we encountered the next extremely strong thermal, the tug vario hit the top stop, moments later it became obvious that the glider was worryingly unstable on tow, a few more moments later I saw the glider in plan form through my rear view mirror and then the rope broke. An immediate 180 degree turn enabled me to see the Pegase going through the most amazing gyrations varying from flat spin through hammerhead stalls. After what seemed like ages the glider hit the ground, next to a thick wooded area in a flat attitude but spinning. I followed it down to the ground to see if the pilot was still in it but after snagging the rope, which I had forgotten about in the heat of the moment, and a thirty foot high fly past I was unsure as to whether he was in the cockpit or not. I made another approach to the field which was long enough to get into but I was unable to land as, through years of ploughing in the same direction, the ground undulated in a series of quite severe humps which were across my prospective landing direction. Pulling up again quickly to find another field it was obvious that I really had only one choice and that was a field with a wood on the undershoot and a trout farm lake on the overshoot. Just as I was totally committed I had a flash thought about getting out of the field again but was really more concerned for the poor glider pilot. The other pilot was contributing "Oh My God" from the right hand seat. After a successful touch down the wing then unloaded and the aircraft sank through a hard earth crust and came to a rapid halt. I jumped out and ran off in the direction of the glider. On my way through a small hamlet I managed to alert the local Fire Service with my "Au secours, au secours" and various other suitable French phrases. On arriving at the glider it was obvious that the pilot was elsewhere. As he was not in the field he had to be in the thick gorse bush wood which was only feet away. Some ten minutes later while being torn to pieces in the gorse I heard a siren approaching and went to the edge of the wood in time to see the glider pilot being whizzed past standing grinning from ear to ear on the back of the fire engine! Presuming he would be taken to the local hospital I sent his partner off to look after him and returned to the Rallye. We duly met up again at Le Blanc, the glider pilot totally undamaged, the partners unable to get a replacement Pegase there and then and so we flew home.

"What had happened was really very simple. When we went through the first thermal the pilot realised that his seat straps were undone and floating past his ears. He then put the stick between his knees and started doing them up. Then we hit the extremely strong thermal which caused him to lose control of the glider and then to be ejected through the canopy..... Luckily, he had done his parachute straps up! I did not see him in the air under the canopy because the glider did not part the rope until some moments later and I immediately locked on to the glider. After an eventful trip home my offer to help them get the replacement glider was quickly countered with the fact that they were now going to buy a trailer!".

Sadly in all sports there are participants who for one reason or another cheat. We did suffer in days of old but with the new recording loggers utilising Global Positioning height, time and location information, this cannot happen again. To the best of my knowledge, only one competitor has ever been thrown out of a World Championship event and he fiddled his turning point photographs. There was a German pilot taking part in the German National Contest who landed in a field, persuaded his crew to de-rig the glider, then to drive on up the course for another hundred kilometres, re-rig in a field and thus he hoped to claim more points for distance. Unfortunately for him, the crew of another competitor saw him land in the first field, drove on but had a puncture a little while later and then were astonished to see the glider sitting fully rigged in the second field. The pilot had his competition licence revoked for ever! Britain had its share of rogues—or to be kind, maybe possibly non-achievers who develop a distinct 'Walter Mitty' persona. There was a celebrated case of malpractice perpetrated by one such who had himself a field day. On 9 May 1972, he announced that he had broken the British Absolute Height and the Gain of Height records. He told the astonished British Gliding world that he was launched at Booker in a Skylark 4 and after climbing in a cu-nb to 27,000 feet, he contacted wave which took him into the stratosphere to a height of 40,600 feet. His claims were duly accepted by the BGA and although our friend seemed very reluctant to discuss certain aspects of his flight, he revelled in the extensive publicity coverage. They do say that the criminal always comes back to the scene of the crime. Our man decided to have another bite of the cherry. He should have remembered Abraham Lincoln's famous speech at Clinton in 1858 in which he said "You can fool all of the people some of the time, and some of the people all of the time, but you cannot fool all the people all of the time".

The first time round, British records; now a few years later, he claimed the World Absolute and Gain of Height records. The Press coverage was even more impressive than the last time, even the Readers Digest printed an article. The first record flight had made a number of pilots uneasy to say the least but this time however, noses around the movement were really twitching, most people agreed that something did not seem right, Roger Barrett, the Chairman of the BGA decided to act and sought the help of Scotland Yard's world famous forensic laboratory to compare and minutely examine the record breaking barograph chart. The official finding was that the trace had been created in a vacuum chamber. That together with additional evidence from Independent Observers resulted in the BGA refusing all the claims, and furthermore expunging the previous records accredited to the gentleman concerned. His FAI Sporting Licence was permanently withdrawn and no further claims for any type of certified gliding performance would ever be approved by the BGA.

There is an interesting sequel to the story which, of course, so my libel lawyer has asked me to state, has no connection with the record claim in any shape or form, or as they always state in the film world 'has no connection with any person dead or alive'. It so happened that a little time after that a trailer complete with the Kestrel inside it, was found burning merrily on the far side of Booker airfield. By a strange coincidence, one of the syndicate partners owning the Kestrel was our friend of the height record affair. But there is more—some weeks later when the Police were dragging the River Thames near Henley looking for a body which they had reason to believe had been hidden there, they found the Kestrel instrument panel and parachute in their net.

Chapter 20

More Heroes

Gliding is a unique sport which stimulates the mind, develops the young and is an addictive drug! It combines four factors which are not present in many, if any other, forms of sport. It is a team sport on the ground as you need your fellow pilots and friends to help you, it is an individual sport in the air. It is a brawn sport on the ground as rigging and manhandling gliders can be hard work, especially if the pilot lands in an unsuitable field which forces him and his crew to carry the machines through heavy plough or over hedges, yet it is a brain sport in the air. After a racing closed circuit flight the pilot will feel mentally and physically tired but always highly elated. Somebody once said that a sport is only a sport if you can kick it, throw it, shoot it, jump it, kill it or watch it. I am delighted that in his eyes ours is not a sport. Surely the definition of sport in its simplest term is one in which man competes against man. We have the added advantage that in gliding, like sailing, that we also compete with, have to understand, interpret and then use weather conditions like few other sports. Gliding also attracts very many varied types of human beings, all of whom are ' doers' rather than 'watchers'.

Regretfully there is not room to write about all of the interesting characters with whom I have shared many a thermal over Britain but a very few must be recorded.

John Stanley Sproule started gliding with the Yorkshire Club in 1929, grew up to join Slingsby Sailplanes where he designed the 'Cadet' and in 1938 together with Flight Lieutenant Bill Murray broke the British Duration Record by hill soaring the Dunstable Downs for 22 hours, 13 minutes and 35 seconds having launched at 4.09am. They hatched a plot to have food and drink lowered to them from another glider but this failed in glorious fashion. The open cockpit Slingsby Falcon 3 side by side two-seater which they were flying, had flying wires attached to the nose of the glider which were attached to the top of the outer wing struts. As their meals were lowered to them, they watched helplessly as invariably the string to which the packet was attached would be deflected past them and thus they had nothing to eat or drink during the whole flight. He must also have been the only pilot in the world to have had a tow behind an aircraft carrier. After the war their Lordships of the Admiralty decreed that not enough was known about the eddies created behind a carrier which made deck landing difficult in certain weathers. John successfully carried out five flights in the prototype Slingsby T.20, one of which was a shoulder launch off the deck into a stiff breeze. It was his interest, drive and determination after building and flying replica models of gliders designed by Sir George Cayley, (1773-1857) the true father of aviation, that created sufficient interest to build a full scale true replica of his man-carrying glider which was the first in the world. Ken Fripp with his team at Southdown Aero Services built this remarkable machine in their workshop at Lasham. Our all-singing and dancing hero Derek Piggott, who could not resist the challenge of a new type, flew it first at Lasham and then for authenticity for the film being made about the inventor, in the actual dale in Yorkshire used by Cayley. Derek flew sitting 'side-saddle' in the boat-shaped fuselage just as Sir George's coachman had been ordered to do all those years ago.

Two of Sproule's inventions merit special attention. The first was his 'Dry swim trainer'. As a naval helicopter pilot and committed glider pilot he was always keen to encourage others to sample the joys of flying. At the Royal Naval Air Station at Ford in Sussex, now an open prison, he welded up a rectangular steel frame which was mounted on a twenty inch wide axle, and a nine foot long steel pole, which could tilt in every plane, was attached in the centre. He then built a twenty foot wing span glider which moved up and down the pole but was attached to a counter weight sliding inside the pole. The whole contraption was towed along the runway behind a Land Rover or some such vehicle and the pilot was taught to 'fly' the glider. It was a tremendous success and introduced many people to flying. Sadly, after John was posted back to sea, a keen, impetuous know-all pulled the stick back too quickly and unfortunately, as the verse in 'Wings for Prudence' says "Had he done his D.I. proper, he would not have come a cropper", as no one had carried out a thorough daily inspection, the wooden restraining plug flew off the top of the pole, like a tappen leaving a bear in early spring, followed closely by the glider!

His other invention in 1953 was the 'Sproule Net'. At that time rescues were carried out by lowering a wire with a strop on the end of it to those being rescued, who then had to work out how to put the strop on. John had the idea of scooping the casualty out of the water and designed his famous net. His plan was to come up behind the person in the water and simply fish them out. While still perfecting the net, he heard that a Fairey Firefly was in trouble and about to ditch. John shot off to intercept and saw the aircraft go into the sea about six miles off Littlehampton. "Within 30 seconds of immersion" John reported "a very surprised pilot was in our net and being winched up to the helicopter where, cold and wet, he sat shivering until we delivered him to the front door of the sick bay at Ford". To test his invention, his WREN assistant, girl sailor or whatever they are called these days, helped out by swimming around out at sea and waiting until John fished. There was a story told that one day he came back to base with a somewhat irate 'civilian' in the net by mistake, but to be fair John always denied the story, albeit with a wry smile!

Major General Anthony Deane-Drummond DSO, MC with two bars is something else—surely the model for the first 'Action man'. Affectionately known as 'the Dean' or 'D-squared', a former British Gliding Champion, he competed in numerous World Championships. He is the real 'father' of gliding at Lasham, who in 1950 stopped the solo training activities of the Army Gliding Club operation at Odiham airfield which had been plagued by numerous accidents. With John Free as the resident instructor and using their new much-loved 'Rudolph', a T.21 with a bright red nose, the club transferred to Lasham in June 1950. He has lived a life fuller than most. His two autobiographies, *Return Ticket* and *Arrows of Fortune*, relate the stories of his extraordinary wartime escapes in Sicily and later after the Arnhem landings where he hid in a cupboard in a German Officers Mess for thirteen days. His account of his time as Commanding Officer of 22 SAS regiment and the capture of a rebel stronghold on a seven thousand foot high mountain in Oman which had never been successfully achieved in recorded history, together with some of his gliding tales make fascinating reading. He is a tough hombre who can make grown men cry, even women, as Ann Welch can testify, but never seems to lose his cool. Except once, as a number of us can confirm.

During one National Championship held at Lasham, Tony DD and Paddy Kearon collided in cloud over Oxford. As DD was then a Brigadier and Paddy only a Group Captain, one rank below, the Dean called it insubordination and worse—an RAF plot to fix the Army! He flew out of cloud and radioed to anyone nearby to give him a report of the damage to the wing of his K.6 single seater. Reassured that only a quarter of one wing was missing, he went back into what had in the meantime developed into a full blown CuNb, turned the first turning point and pressed on to South Marston near Swindon for his second control point. By now the thunderstorm had killed off all the lift and with lots of others he was forced to land at South Marston airfield. For the first and only time I heard him curse and swear so vehemently that we wondered what would happen when he and Paddy next met but he pointed out that he was not concerned about the air to air, what really got to him was that all he wanted was one more good climb so that he could have got back to base to complete the task.

Real champions have to be totally dedicated with a fierce determination to win. One of these giants was Sir Peter Scott, the creator of the Severn Wildfowl Trust and the splendid World Wild Life campaign to protect endangered species, artist of note, sailor, and lots more besides who took to gliding like his beloved ducks do to water. He left nothing to chance, his attention to detail was awe inspiring. Everyone was keen to sit next to him at briefing or later when he took on the mantle of Chairman of the British Gliding Association as any piece of paper near him would invariably be covered with drawings of ducks. He had a lively, sometimes wicked, sense of humour and delighted in leaving in the cockpit a phoney list of coded position points to be radioed to his crew during Championships knowing full well that other pilots would slavishly copy them down. Then it was important to keep your crew informed of your location and prospects, without giving valuable information to your competitors, so that they could follow you as closely as possible in case of an out-landing followed by the mad rush back for a re-light. On one 300km task during the Aston Down National Championships, Peter and I were approaching the first turning point at Cerne Abbas in Dorset. A little later I called up "Mallard, KanKan, I can't see the naked giant" and back came Peter's radio message "KanKan, Mallard, you are now directly overhead his left testicle". Every pilot listening out on 130.4 had a good laugh—for those of you who have never seen the imposing figure of the Giant which was carved in the hillside allegedly many hundred years ago—it is a grand sight but not to be undertaken with an aged maiden aunt in tow.

One other hero must also be remembered. He was Fred Slingsby. Philip Wills described him as was the most widely loved man I have known. 'Sling' was a wonderful character, full of humour, a man of real enterprise who designed and built beautiful and highly successful sailplanes which found favour throughout the world. During the First World War he had been awarded the Military Medal for a remarkable feat. The pilot of his aircraft had been fatally injured by anti-aircraft fire and Fred climbed from his observer/gunner's position over the fuselage and successfully flew the machine back to his base sitting on the body of his pilot. After the war 'Sling' returned to coffin and furniture making in Scarborough and when the gliding bug bit him in the early 1930s, he designed and built his first machine. At the same time, to help keep the many visitors to the town entertained, he built a fleet of assorted wooden warships which re-enacted famous sea battles. Each ship was propelled by a man sitting inside it, pedalling like mad to turn the underwater screw and from time to time also fired a gun at the hapless enemy who always lost. When asked about the glider factory his answer was "I make machines in which people can throw themselves over a cliff —time and time again!"

In the nineteen-thirties with the help of a public spirited wealthy Yorkshire land owner, Major Jack Shaw, he started 'Slingsby Sailplanes of Kirbymoorside. When anyone asked him to explain his design methods, he would say "I whittle a piece of wood and when I have done whittling, I build it and fly it." His all-time high was the 'Sky, which in 1952 won the World Gliding Championships in Spain with Philip Wills as its pilot, and swept the board with 3rd, 4th, 7th, 9th, 11th and 13th places as well. I sent him a telegram which read "Well whittled with wood, you wonderful wizard" which 'Fluff', his delightful wife, said he much appreciated. When you visited the factory to order your new glider, he took you to lunch in a scruffy pub in the village of Kirbymoorside. When you went to collect your new pride and joy, he treated you to a sumptuous meal at that socially OK establishment, the Black Swan in Helmsley, known as the 'Mucky Duck', but only if you brought your cheque with you! The Shaw-Slingsby Trust, an unsuccessful financial dalliance, not of 'Sling's' making, followed by two consecutive take-overs virtually finished off the last British glider manufacturing unit and there has been no quantity production in this country since.

Another never to be forgotten hero, although only an ' adopted' Lashamite, was Lefty Kurylowicz. A fighter pilot during the war, after being shot down he spent thirteen days in an open dinghy drifting ever closer to the coast of France and was rescued in the nick of time. He had been awarded Poland's highest medal for bravery and remained in the Royal Air Force after the end of the war. Some time in the fifties, an injury to his spine which temporarily left him bent almost double saw him installed at Headley Court, the

RAF Rest and Recuperation Centre. One day another patient arrived there called Theo McEvoy, later a Vice President of the BGA. Air Chief Marshal Sir Theodore McEvoy, when only 23, was two years out of the RAF College Cranwell where he had won the Sword of Honour when doctors detected ankylosing spondylitis, a progressive, crippling disease of the spine. In spite of the pain and disability, he carved out a brilliant career which made him a legend in the Air Force. In 1941 when he was given command of RAF Northolt, the home of the Polish Fighter Wing, he took every opportunity to lead his pilots into battle. Later that year he was shot down over the French coast but was able to nurse his Hurricane back before crash landing at Lydd, albeit in the middle of a minefield from which he was only rescued the next day. Due to his deformed spine which made him walk with a serious stoop, he was sent to Headley Court for some well earned rest. The morning Lefty and he met, Lefty had just collected a plate of porridge when he came forehead to forehead with Theo who was about to do the same. "Please" said Lefty "who is taking the mickey out of whom?". With their impish sense of humour, the common love of flying and gliding, and Theo's affection for his Polish pilots who had recently invested him as a Commander of the Order of Polonia Restituta, they forged an instantaneous friendship. In RAFGSA Contests they flew in a two-seater whenever possible. Lefty tells a story about one flight which was not going to plan. "The thermals don't like us, we get lower and lower and things look bad. Theo say Land. I say No. He say—Land. I say No. He say—I am Air Chief Marshal, you only Flight Lieutenant, I say—land. So I say—On ground you big boss, me little fish. In air me big boss, you little fish, we go on".

Lefty will always be remembered for the tale concerning his brother who had left the Air Force to try his luck in the world outside. When they met Lefty said "Hello, Mr. Civilian Kurylowicz". "No Lefty, Now no more Kurylowicz, but Brown". "Brown" said Lefty "our father he turn in his grave". "Look, in the Air Force with fellow Poles, our name is no problem. Now in civilian life people ask my name and when I tell them, they say please spell. So I am fed up and change. Now no one will ask how you spell Brown". Three months later Lefty met his brother again and said "Hello Mr. Brown". "No, not Brown—Smith". "Smith?" asked Lefty. His brother said "Lefty, when I say my name is Brown, they say but you have Polish accent, what your name before. When I tell them, they ask how you spell. Now I am Mr. Smith. When they say but you have Polish accent, what was your name before, I say Brown and nobody ask silly question".

John Hunt of Everest fame, Derek Piggott, Philip Wills and Ann Welch

Dear Ann Welch loved sending us to Perranporth

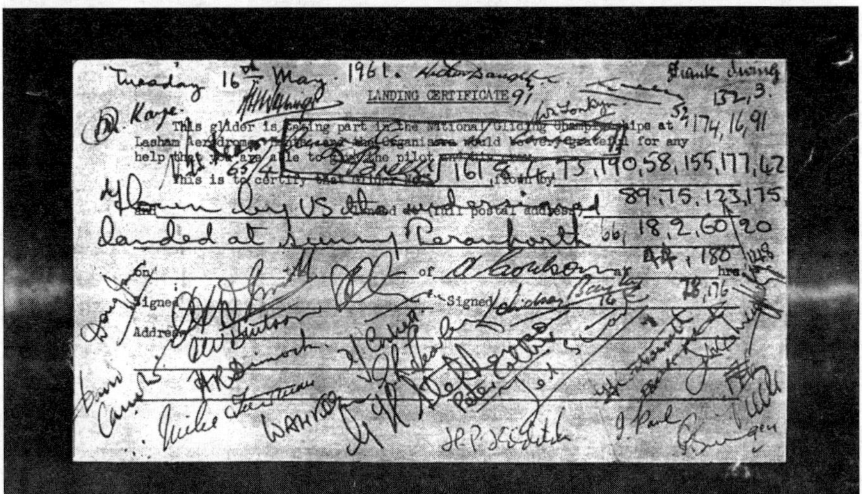

Tuesday 16th May. 1961.

LANDING CERTIFICATE 91

This glider is taking part in the National Gliding Championships at Lasham Aerodrome, and the Organisers would be very grateful for any help that you are able to give the pilot

This is to certify that glider No. 161 ... from by

and landed at (full postal address)

landed at Sunny Perranporth

on of at hrs.

Signed Signed

Address

174, 16, 91

190, 58, 155, 177, 62

89, 75, 123, 175

66, 18, 2, 60, 20

180

176

Chapter 21

And finally

Gliding is a way of life second to none. Every pilot will describe his flights in graphic detail and a talented few including Philip Wills had the ability to write quite lyrical books about the sport which are highly recommended. Whenever glider pilots meet, of whatever nationality, even in far flung places in the world, they invariably find that they have much in common. Although the weather conditions they meet and the terrain over which they fly will not be the same, the challenge, the sheer joy of soaring high in the sky and the sense of achievement after a good flight is very much the same. Even after a fraught flight when the famous saying of 'I'd rather be down here looking up there, rather than being up there looking down here' is appropriate, moments of apprehension or mild fear are soon forgotten and you cannot wait to get airborne again.

The business of finding keen, hard working members to keep the club operations going is not a problem as there is happily a constant stream of eager early pilots who appreciate that their progress in the sport will be enhanced by their efforts and the efforts of others. Finding well qualified mature committee members is however an increasing worry as the pressures of earning a living become more acute and leave less and less time and energy to devote to the complex commercial demands made by the efficient running of a Club.

Philip Wills in *Free as a Bird* makes much of the need to create a firm structure within the Movement in order to ensure success. Writing in the Royal Aeronautical Society's Centenary Journal in 1966, Philip Wills wrote " Perhaps the next vital question to be answered was whether or no the first band of pioneers would find a second wave to carry on the torch. The twenty years since the end of the war have provided an affirmative answer. People like........., and many others show that there are still challenges sufficiently difficult and enticing to attract people of the calibre required...".

Now as the end of the century nears, we must ensure that the third, fourth and future waves will be stimulated to the same extent. The triple dangers of selfishness, mammonism and personal hedonism which modern life seems to encourage in some must be fought and defeated at all costs. At the very time when new pupils are not as thick on the ground as formerly, when increasingly oppressive legislation is threatened and the scales of the movement may have tipped too far in favour of the quest for podium positions against all the others who still provide the larger share of a club's income. It is absolutely imperative that 'people of the calibre required' are found, nurtured and encouraged to take a longer view if our sport we know and love it is to survive.

Nevertheless, the new technology of Global Positioning System instruments which detail the height, position and time coupled with the loggers which record and store this information to be downloaded and later analysed together with highly sophisticated electronic variometers which give the pilot detailed information about the very airmass in which he flies has immeasurably enhanced high performance gliding. These advances open up even greater opportunities to explore new soaring terrain throughout the world but also sharpen up competitions to a remarkable extent. They, coupled with the very latest development in sailplane design make the future exciting and will keep the sport at the forefront of man's endeavour.

Lorne Welch's favourite expression was "Don't just stand there, DO something!". I am the first to admit that some people did not always agree with some of my 'somethings'. Philip Wills in *Free as a Bird* described me over one matter as a Bull in a China Shop. Barbara Carrow claims that "Wally is brilliant at pouring oil on troubled waters—and then setting light to it". Justified criticism I fully accept. To people making less helpful comments, I say "You do better, then come back and I'll listen".

The problems of squaring the circle—this being the family, work and the sport, is the ever present balancing trick which glider pilots must learn as early as possible. I am ashamed to admit that to date during fifty four years of continuous gliding, I have only been on two non-gliding holidays each lasting only one week! Such is obsession! Over the many years I have been very fortunate to part own some fabulous gliders, flown many hours and miles cross-country and broken a few records. As well as competing in numerous championships, directing and task setting, I have completed more than 11,000 tows as a tug pilot. Obsession does bring ample rewards!

An on-going quirk of keen pilots whenever they are travelling, especially by train, is that each field as it is passed is carefully analysed for the surface and crops, best direction of approach for landing and any obvious obstructions which might prove to be a hazard. Also 'Spaghetti Western' films are highly unpopular with the gliding fraternity as night shots are so obviously shot during the day using a special filter as there are always beautiful cumulus clouds filling in the sky, something which the angel in charge of weather never arranges for us at night.

I have been remarkably lucky in my chosen sport. The flying and the wide spread of administrative jobs that have come my way have all been hugely enjoyable. The certain knowledge that I was able to put back more into the sport than I took out gives me satisfaction which will last even in my old age when active participation has come to a full stop.

Aeons ago, when I was courting my wife, we went to a cinema to see some now long forgotten film. As the climax of the love story was reached, just as the hero was about to take the heroine in his arms for their first passionate kiss, I am told that I turned to my future bride and said "My God, just look at that sky!". For evermore she said "If only I had realised the full significance of that remark, I would have got up and run!" I am forever grateful that she didn't.

Is there really enough room for you in there?

'WINGS FOR PRUDENCE'

or 'The death of a Snooper' — a melodrama

A sordid tale of love and treachery, first produced at Redhill in 1949

Cast:
Chief Flying Instructor
Prudence, his daughter
Prune, the Hero
Dishforth, the villain

The action takes place in a Chief Flying Instructor's office, all the time.

Scene 1: Morning
Enter CFI and Prudence.

CFI: *Oh Prudence dear, what can we do,*
This club will drive me crazy
These careless clots have pranged the lot
And left us only Daisy.
PRUE: *We must keep calm*
Unlike that club in Surrey,
They've pranged themselves as well you know
So I say 'Not to worry'.
CFI: *We must quickly raise some money*
Otherwise we've had it honey.
PRUE: *A little course is what we need*
Attracting here the Bulldog breed
CFI: *A fine idea! I'll now address*
An advert to the local press,
One other thing is rather fraught
As we've done what we didn't ought
We must continue the evasion,
Of accident investigation.

Exeunt.

Scene 2: A week later

Enter Prudence. Tidies up.
Noise of ancient motor car.
Enter Prune followed by Dishforth.

PRUNE: *Excuse me miss,*
Is this,
The West Downs Gliding Club?
PRUE: *But yes!*
And now I'd rather
You waited here while I get father

Exit Prue

PRUNE: (aside) *If it takes me half my life,*
That lovely girl must be my wife.
DISHFORTH: (aside)
The best technique with this young flower
Is a low approach and bags of power.

Enter CFI and Prudence.

CFI: *Good morning Chaps,*
You want to try To learn to fly.
PRUNE: *Indeed I do,*
But though I've seen some years in Burma
I've never yet left terra firma.
CFI TO DISH: *Tell me, my son,*
Have you ever flown before?
DISHFORTH: *A mere twelve thousand hours or more,*
But every one was in the war.
I've flown through cu-nimbs by the score
And bailing out is just a bore
I find this office rather trying
Let's go out and do some flying.
CFI: *Good! I too find it rather boring,*
I'll go out and do some soaring

Exeunt CFI and DISH

PRUNE: *Prudence—excuse my hasty action*
But I love you to distraction.
I can take you from all this

	Off to endless nuptial bliss.
	Darling do not think me mad
	Tell me—'Can I ask your Dad?'.
PRUE:	*Marry you!*
	You've not a hope,
	You haven't yet gone solo dope.

Exit Prue

PRUNE:	*If at first you blunder slightly,*
	Try again, but more politely

Exit Prune

Scene 3: Later that day

Enter CFI and Dish

CFI:	*Good show; I'm glad to say*
	I think you're doing nicely
	To-morrow morn you start at dawn
	That's five o'clock precisely.
DISH:	*Am I shortly to be sent on an unaccompanied ascent?*
CFI:	*You can do a solo flight*
	To-morrow if the wind is right.
DISH:	*What's the betting that it ceases,*
	But what on earth are all these pieces?
CFI:	*Jimmy here got in a spin,*
	Less a rather vital pin.
	Little Francis ever proud,
	Passed on in a thunder cloud.
	Harry had five grand at Dover
	This seat alone got safely over.
	That is only half the story
	Of our club's undoubted glory,
	But widespread consternation
	And ministerial measures
	Would follow publication
	Of our destructive pleasures.
DISH:	*Not a whisper will I utter.*
	Not a mention, not a mutter.

CFI: *To such an upright man as you,*
I would gladly give my Pru.

Exit CFI

DISH: *What a simple little man*
Never to suspect my plan
Of persons I am no respecter
Of accidents I'm Chief Inspector.

(enter PRUNE unseen)

PRUNE: *You villain Sir! You wretched cad!*
You'll part a damsel from her Dad,
If the Minister hears this tale
The CFI will go to gaol.
Disguising an official
I'll not hesitate to say
For processes judicial
Is not the British way.

DISH: *Was not the British way.*
You can save the whole position,
If you'll accept my one condition,
That it's clearly understood
You abandon Prue for good.
The prang rate I have found
Can be quietly scrubbed around.

PRUNE: *I must perforce agree*
To your infernal plot
For she'll never marry me
If her Father's on the spot.

DISH: *Good show! I must now depart*
You've saved the girl a broken heart

(Exit laughing)

PRUNE: *I can quickly turn the tables,*
And fix this wretched traitor
By filing through the cables of Daisy's elevator

(Exit. Filing noises off)

Scene 4: The next morning

Enter CFI, PRUNE and DISHFORTH

CFI: *All ready Chaps,*
We must press on this morning,
And though the weather's Q.B.I.
I see no reason not to fly
If Uxbridge gets no warning.
For to-days' inaugural flight
You, DISHFORTH, must get ready.
This binding fog obscures the sight

(Prompter blows chalk onto stage)

So take it fairly steady.
The D.I.ing of Daisy is something I should do
But as you're going to fly her
I leave it all to you.
The usual structural defects
You had better overlook
Just twang the wires and bang the tyres.
And sign up in the book

Exeunt

ALL: *Take up slack ... all out.* (Offstage)
Look out he's going to crash

(Sounds of launching and crash off-stage)

Enter PRUNE

PRUNE: *Stupid DISHFORTH never feared*
That his wires were panacea'd,
He would not have come a cropper
Had he done his D.I. proper

CFI: *That DISHFORTH was a bounder,*
He deserves to burn in Hell
In a furnace stoked with plywood
From a primary's nacelle.
Young fellow your devotion
Has been constant brave and true
And so I give permission
For you to woo my PRUE.
And now complete destruction
Of this damned abomination

Leaves me in peace to measure
In metres feet and inches
The complicated stresses
Of automatic winches.

Exit CFI

Enter PRUE

PRUE: *In this situation parlous,*
Darling you've been simply marvellous
Dirty DISHFORTH pranged and dead
Now we can truly wed.

PRUNE: *Quickly, fill your suitcase*
With all essential junk
And forthwith go and park it
In the Club's best bridal bunk.
For tedious wedding details
We have no time to wait
In the Club's new whitewashed workshop
We have an urgent date.
The timely death of DISHFORTH
Has saved you boundless shame
Now reconstructing Daisy
Is our most pressing aim.

Exeunt

The End

A small selection of various Club's Songs are worthy of inclusion.

He wrapped it up round a tree in a claptrap
Surrey Club
Words by Pat Wood
Tune: Tarpaulin Jack

He wrapped it up round a tree in a claptrap
He pulled the wings off in a dive
He stove in the bulkheads on landing
And hoped no one saw him arrive
He pulled back the stick on the take-off
And wiped the tail off on the ground
He broke it in so many pieces
That half of them never were found
He landed the thing in a tree top
And had to be rescued by crane
Then he took the remaining club glider
And went round and did it again
Said the CFI, grieving and sorrowful
"Now I realise you couldn't care less
But you might be a little more careful
You've put all our gliders U/S"
Said the pilot "Oh bloody good show, chaps
It's just what I wanted to do
For now that we've finished with flying
We can play with my little canoe".

Air streams warm and unstable
Surrey Club
Words by B.T.
Tune: All Things Bright and Beautiful

Chorus
Air streams warm and un-stable
With Cu-Nims great and small
Sailplanes clapped and runcible
We're no damn good at all

We fly Gold C cross-country
With nothing but a bun
We're frozen sick and weary
Yes, Gliding is such fun

We tried to soar the mountains
And landed mid the peaks
A mountain goat was hostile
We couldn't sit for weeks

We tried the competitions
But soon had had our fill
We needed flies not sailplanes
With 50 on the hill

We did some sea-breeze research
And drifted out to sea
We couldn't catch a thermal
But caught some fish for tea

Less famous clubs pay visits
They have a smashing day
And when they go at nightfall
We clear the bits away

So now we've no more gliders
Let's concentrate on beer
We've had enough of fraughtness
To last us many a year

We've lost our last Olympia
A clot without a clue
Observed the red ball rising
And thought he'd go up too

Final Chorus:
Air streams warm and un-stable

Strong west winds at Dunstable
We leave it all to you
We're going to the Zoo

God rest you merry gentlemen
Surrey Club
Words by Pat Wood
Tune as the Hymn

God rest you merry gentlemen, let nothing you dismay
The Clubhouse will not always look the way it looks to-day
Prospective members will not merely shrug and drive away
We'll have gliding in comfort and joy

One day we'll have four poster beds and scented sheets as well
And lots of pretty waitresses to ring the dinner bell
We'll have news letters edited by people who can spell
We'll have gliding in comfort and joy

We'll win the National Competitions every year with ease
And all our Daisy customers will have their Silver 'C's
And when we go cross country, we'll be issued with rupees
We'll have gliding in comfort and joy

All other clubs will be as friendly as can be
The Editors of Gliding magazines will all agree
That expensive German gliders should be given to us free
We'll have gliding in comfort and joy

Now when all this has come to pass as in good time it may
And when at last we've found a way to make our gliding pay
We'll go and start another club a long long way away
You can have too much comfort and joy

The Lashamite Song
Lasham Gliding Society

To the gliders down at Lasham, to the tug planes and the cars
To the poor old battered hangar where they dwell
Sing the Lashamites assembled with their glasses raised on high
And the magic of their singing casts a spell.
Yes the magic of their singing of the songs we love so well
Competitions, held at SPLASHAM, bloody hell!
We will sing our songs of gliding, while life and voice shall last
Then we'll pass and be forgotten like the rest.

Chorus:
We're poor little lambs who have lost our way, baa, baa, baa
We're little black sheep who have gone astray, baa, baa, baa
Gentlemen pilots out on a spree, doomed from here to eternity
Lord have mercy on such as we, baa, baa, baa

To the writers of the log sheets, to the trailers and their crews
To the tow cars which the members drive like hell
Sing the Lashamites assembled with their glasses raised on high
And the magic of their singing casts a spell
Yes the magic of their singing of the songs we love so well
The Yew Tree, Golden Pottie and the rest
We will serenade our Derek who flies until the last
Then we'll pass and be forgotten like the rest

Chorus

To the members in the bunkhouse, and in their caravans
To the elsans in their hut complete with smell
Sing the Lashamites assembled with their glasses raised on high
And the magic of their singing casts a spell
Yes the magic of their singing of the songs we love so well
You name it, Jill will sing it by request
We will serenade old Wally whose gliding days are past
Then we'll pass and be forgotten like the rest

Chorus

To the toilers in the kitchen, to the barrels full of beer
To the stories in the bar we love to tell
Sing the Lashamites assembled with their glasses raised on high
And the magic of their singing casts a spell
Yes the magic of their singing, of the songs we love so well
The remaining songs have had to be suppressedË
We will serenade each other till the bar shall close at last
Then we'll say good night and pass out like the rest

He had to go and prang it in a claptrap
Surrey Club
Words by Hugo Trotter
Tune: She had to go and lose it at the Astor.
Note: This song is intended as a solo effort and not for massed bar voices

We'd like to tell you the story of a young pilot about 22, about 5 feet 10 inches and about to go away. Now his Instructor, realising it was the first time he was to go on a cross country, called him to the office and said—"Jimmy, you're all dressed up in your finery, with your brand new Olympia and your thermal hat and you look lovely. Now I want you to remember everything I have ever told you and above all I want you to be very, very careful".

But he had to go and prang it in a claptrap
Forgetting his Instructor's good advice
He landed it obliquely to the furrows
And now he finds he'll have to pay the price
He telephoned the clubhouse in a hurry
To get someone to come and fetch him back
And when they all returned home in the evening
They found the C.F.I. there, looking black

'Why did you go and prang it in a claptrap?
There's really very little I can say

We'll go and write an accident report out
And send it forthwith to the B.G.A.'

The B.G.A. received it with amazement
They weren't exactly sure just what to do
The Chairman said 'The last time that we had one
Was in the Spring of 1932'

'Why must they go and prang them in a claptrap
Why can't they learn to land a cheaper way?
I think the proper action at this juncture
Is to write a letter to the C.A.A.

A postcard came back promptly in a fortnight
To tell them that their letter was received
They had been thinking somebody had lost it
So most of them sat down and were relieved

Dear Sirs, Why must you prang them in a claptrap
Please forward us the Pilot straight away
We think the Minister would like to see him
It's too serious for any more delay

The Pilot turned up early in the morning
Sincerely wishing that he had been dead
But as they helped him through the open doorway
The Minister arose and this he said

'I hear you went and pranged it in a claptrap
To me it seems remarkably amiss
But seeing I know nothing about flying
I don't know why they bother me with this'

'So go back to your club and do not worry
My sympathies are with you, my dear chap
And next time that you fly, you must really have a try
To prang another in another claptrap'.

Bloody gliding weather
London Gliding Club
Tune: Eton Boating Song

Bloody Gliding Weather
Inversion at forty feet
The reason it isn't raining
The rain has turned to sleet
So we will all get drunk together
On watered down Dunstable beer
If we have to go gliding some where
Why the hell do we have to come here?

Lovely gliding weather
A cracking five hundred day
So the tug pilots are leaving the action
By putting the tugs away
You can't get away from a winch launch
So you're stuck in the bar drinking beer
If we have to go gliding somewhere
Why the hell do we have to come here?

Lovely gliding weather
You can soar the hill in a sedan
But you can't have excess of pleasure
So we will slap on a hundred hour ban
Its' easy enough to hill soar
If half the club's taken out of the air
If we have to go gliding somewhere
Why the hell do we have to come here?

Lousy gliding weather
You can't see the hill for the fog
So we're spending the time making money
Selling off the manure from the dogs
We've had written complaints from the pig farm
That we are badly polluting the air

If we have to go gliding somewhere
Why the hell do we have to come here?

The Slingsby serenade

Yorkshire Club
Tune: The Penny Serenade

Once we strayed to the workshop of a famous Sailplane maker
And he smiled when the contents of our trailer we displayed
"See, See, See, can you mend it, Mister Slingsby?"
"S'truth" said he, "What a horrid mess you've made"
From his eye shone that tender light that hinted much repairing
And we sighed, for we wondered if he ever could be paid
"Si, Si Si, it's quite easy, Mister Slingsby
See, See, See, all these little bits we've saved"
You may guess 'twas a mess, every part had been broken
And our crew, they were blue, for loud oaths had been spoken
Still we feel that when Sling has done the job we shall remember
In his heart he will always feel more happy when he's paid
See, See, See, what a topping job he's made
And the trouble we've been saved
And the bill....
Will it be paid?

The Twelve Days at Lasham

Lasham Gliding Society
Tune: The Twelve Days of Christmas

"On the ------ day at Lasham my instructor said to me..."

12 This thing flies itself. Look All you have to do it to make it go where you want it to....so

1 Put the nose down
Pull the knob twice
1 Look round first
Now turn left

Don't forget the rudder…left foot…OTHER foot!

1 Keep the nose up

Watch the horizon

Look! There's Alton

1 Let's do a stall

Full opposite rudder (pause)

Forward on the stick

Back to normal flight

1 Increase your speed

2 Ignore the altimeter

3 HAND ON THE BRAKE

4 Straighten up now

5 Wings level and

6 Look well ahead

7 Keep it floating as long as you can

The Met Song

Surrey Club

Words by Anon

Tune: I'm in love with a wonderful guy

Some folks study neurology
Technical ethics or Spanish mythology
Me, I'm an expert in meteorology
Just 'cos I'm learning to fly

Chorus

Warm fronts and cold fronts, depressions, occlusions
I'm perfectly sure met. men suffer delusions
For they always draw the wrong conclusions
They haven't a clue, how or why

You may think the met man's a bit of a clot
But I am informed that he knows quite a lot
Though all I can say is "God only knows what"
For it hasn't yet reached you or I

They look down with scorn on the old Shepherd's warning
And say that it's bound to be fine in the morning
And then when it's raining like hell with the dawning
They say the humidity's high

Dunstable said that the cu-nimbs would grow
So Lorne declared Strasbourg and started to go
But he landed at Farnham in three feet of snow
And he dented his wonderful Sky

Met men pronounced it would be a dull day
So we sent off a pupil to try for his 'A'
He made a spot landing in Botany Bay
We retrieved him by way of Shanghai

They're quite sure there's fog on the Cornish Riviera
A heatwave in Lapland and snow in Madeira
But when you enquire what it's going to do here –
"er It may rain – it may remain dry"

Pine cones and seaweed are no use at all
So throw them away and give Larkhill a call
For though all their forecasts may mean b----r all
Well, at least you'll admit that they try

The Daisy list
Surrey Club
Words B.H.
Tune: The Lincolnshire Poacher

When I was young I longed to be
A glider pilot bold
To join the joyous company
(Like Arthur's knights of old)
Of men who wear the shining C 2
Of silver and of gold

I took myself to a gliding club
And saw the C.F.I.
He said 'We work so hard round here
We haven't the strength to fly
But we'll put your name on the Daisy list
And let you have a try

I took the Tutor away one day
And landed it in a tree
It met another Tutor there
And raised a family
So-o put me back on the Daisy list
For that's the place for me

For fifteen and three-quarter hours
I lingered on the hill
The hill was high and so was I
Or I'd have been there still
But they put me back on the Daisy list
Until I paid the bill

In search of height I took the Kite
A cu-nim tall inside
And at the top St.Peter sat
And laughed until he cried
And he said 'You will never come here again
But I'll tell the Lord you tried
Yes, you'd better get back on the Daisy list
And tell them how you died

The Committee Dittee

Surrey Club

Oh, ain't it a pity we are the Committee that runs this mammoth show
They tried to dislodge us but they couldn't budge us—we just refused to go
We're the oldest of firms on Christian name terms with Wills and Basil Meads
Lloyd George we knew the Goodharts too and all the pre war-seeds
We keep the Club on good behaviour
They're all in bed by half past ten
We used to have quite rowdy parties
But can promise they won't occur again

We set you all a good example because we're socially okay
Dining apart with a bottle of wine
To sleep with the others we firmly decline
We must stand on our dignity, come what may

And yet we must uphold democracy
So at every A.G.M.
The other member re-elects me
And I reciprocate by re-electing him

So night and day that's how we labour
We never slack and never laze
We use up the rest of our valuable time
Indulging a talent for scurrilous rhyme
Making up libellous, wicked and tactless plays

I'm a little Bungey Flower

Source: Glider Pilot's Psalter Derby & Lancs Club
Tune: I'm a Little Prairie Flower

The "Grunau" is so beautiful
The "H-Seventeen" so small
The "Falcon Three" so wonderful
Why can't I soar them all?

Chorus

Oh I'm a little Bungey Flower
Growing bolder every hour
Nobody cares about my 'B'
So wait till I show you my Silver 'C'
To-day from two
I had to wildly dash
I hid behind a Primary
And whispered Crash! Crash! Crash!

The boys give me the glad-eye
And they say I'm rather cute
But I'm a little devil
When I'm in my flying suit

Instructors are all so kind to me
And dearly love to chat
And last night in the hangar
Well, that's quite enough of that

On rainy days we all get wet
Though soaked we never tire
So the lads help me to dry my smalls
In front of the Club House fire

My young man's a Pilot bold
And loves to go a-soaring
With his parachute and joystick cute
New sites he goes exploring

Oh this Gliding's simply gorgeous
It keeps your nerves so cool
I've learnt a lot of useful tricks
Not taught in Sunday School

You can't stop me from gliding

Derby & Lancs Club
Tune: Can't Stop Me from Dreaming

You can stop me from loving you
You can stop me from cuddling too
You can stop my beer money, that's all right
But you'll sleep by yourself on Saturday night
'Cause you can't stop me from gliding

You can stop me from holding hands
You can even forbid the banns
You can say "No, No, Honey" that's all right
But you won't see me 'till Sunday night
Cause I'm at Camphill Gliding

I've just got to be, in the air so free
Come up and see, just what it means to me
You can divorce me just as you choose
Burn all my togs dear, my boots and shoes
In my birthday suit I'll look quite swell
Sailing along in the old Nacelle,
'Cause that's OK in gliding

BIBLIOGRAPHY

List of books published in the United Kingdom

Ashwell-Cooke	*Motorless flight;* 1932 J Hamilton
Blanchard	*Elementary gliding;* 1955, B.G.A.
Bradbury	*Meteorology and flight;* 1991 A & C Black
Brown	*Wings of the weird & wonderful;* 1983 Oldbourne
Butler	*War Prizes;* 1994 Midland Publishing
Cumming	*The powerless ones;* 1966 Frederick Muller
Deane-Drummond	*Arrows of fortune;* 1992 Leo Cooper
Deane-Drummond	*Return ticket;* 1953 Collins
Delafield	*Gliding competitively;* 1982 A & C Black
Dittmer	*A study from a glider pilot's experience;* 1938 Macmillan
Douglas (Welch)	*Cloud reading for pilots;* 1943 John Murray
Edmonds (Welch)	*Silent flight;* 1939 Country Life
Ellison	*British gliders and sailplanes 1922/70;* 1971 A & C Black
Embry	*Mission completed;* 1957 Methuen
Entwistle	*The met. aspects of gliding flight;* 1931 Aeronautical Society
Flanders & Carr	*Gliding and motorless flight;* 1930 Isaac Pitman
Fox Green	*The ABC of gliding;* 1952 Geo. Allen & Unwin
Gotch	*Playground in the sky;* 1955 Hutchinson
Hardy	*Gliders and sailplanes of the world;* 1982 Ian Allen
Horsley	*The long flight;* 1947 Country Life Ltd
Horsley	*Soaring flight;* 1944 Eyre & Spottiswoode
Ince	*Combat and competition;* 1992 Newton
Irving	*The paths of soaring flight;* 1998 Imperial College Press
Jackson	*Tiger in the sky;* 1997 Pat Jackson
Jane's	*World sailplanes and motor gliders:* 1978 Jane's
Kahn	*A glider pilot bold......;* 1998 Jardine Publishing
Kronfeld	*Kronfeld on gliding and soaring;* 193? John Hamilton

Kukuski	*Theory and technique of soaring;* 193? Issac Pitman
Latimer Needham	*Gliding and soaring;* 1935 Philip Allan
Latimer Needham	*Sailplanes*; 1937 Chapman and Hall
Lomax	*Hanna Reitsch*; 1988 John Murray
Meagher	*Chicken-hearted granny;* 1987 Ava Books
Millett	*Teaching Harry to fly;* 1994 Hartley Publishers
Mole	*Happy landings;* 1984 Airlife
Morison	*Flak and ferrets;* 1995 Sentinel Publishing
Pilcher	*Gliding;* 1910 Aeronautical Society
Piggott	*Beginning gliding;* 1975 A & C Black
Piggott	*Delta Papa;* 1977 Pelham
Piggott	*Derek Piggott on gliding;* 1990 A & C Black
Piggott	*Gliding, a handbook on soaring flight;* 1958 A & C Black
Piggott	*Gliding safety;* 1991 A & C Black
Piggott	*Going solo;* 1978 A & C Black
Piggott	*Understanding flying weather;* 1988 A & C Black
Piggott	*Understanding gliding;* 1977 A & C Black
Pudney	*A Pride of Unicorns;* 1960 Oldbourne
Richardson	*Wingless victory;* 1954 Odhams
Scott	*The eye of the wind;* 1961 Hodder and Stoughton
Scull	*Gliding and soaring;* 1977 Pelham
Serjeant & Watson	*The gliding book;* 1965 Nichola Kaye
Simons	*Slingsby sailplanes;* 1996 Airlife
Simpson	*Tackle gliding this way;* 1961 Stanley Paul
Sitek and Blunt	*Gliding and soaring;* 1940 Alliance Press
Sproule	*Gliding and power flying*; 1947 O.U.P.
Stafford-Allen	*Theory of flight for glider pilots;* 1962 Oliver and Boyd
Stamer and Lippisch	*Gliding and sail-planing;* 1930 Bodley Head
Stewart	*The glider pilot's manual;* 1994 Airlife
Wallington	*Meteorology for glider pilots;* 1961 John Murray
Weiss	*Gliding and soaring flight;* 193? Sampson Low
Welch	*Come gliding with me;* 1955 Fred. Muller
Welch	*Complete soaring guide;* 1986 A & C Black
Welch	*Glider flying;* 1963 Constable
Welch	*Gliding and advanced soaring;* 1947 John Murray

Welch	*Happy to fly;* 1983 John Murray
Welch	*John goes gliding;* 1964 Jonathan Cape
Welch	*KTG gliding;* 1994 A & C Black
Welch	*The story of gliding;* 1980 John Murray
Welch, Welch & Irving	*The soaring pilot;* 1955 John Murray
Welch, Welch & Irving	*The new soaring pilot;* 1970 John Murray
Wills	*On being a bird;* 1953 Max Parrish
Wills	*Free as a bird;* 1973 William Clowes
Wills	*Where no birds fly;* 1961 Newnes
Wright	*Wooden sword;* 1967 Elek Books

Index